dining room
mirrored wall
metal tie bars, also option without these curtains
honey coloured wood console with glass shelf & maybe lighting incorporated under top
bois très clair
ferronnerie special
acajou
inlay blue lacquer or ivory?
red suede
75 cm
60 cm
45 cm
88
103
pied en plan
traversin
2.50
bois foncé
86 cm
47 (assise)
98
roulettes

TINO
ZERVUDACHI

TINO ZERVUDACHI

A PORTFOLIO

Natasha Fraser-Cavassoni

Editorial director: Suzanne Slesin
Design: Stafford Cliff
Managing editor: Regan Toews
Production: Dominick J. Santise, Jr.
Assistant editor: Deanna Kawitzky

POINTED LEAF PRESS, LLC.
WWW.POINTEDLEAFPRESS.COM

Contents

Preface

I have known Tino since he was a child. In those far-gone days, he sparkled with curiosity and joy. The star-like quality and bundle of energy was as apparent then as it is today. I can remember him for a lark and a bit of pocket-money, acting out the role of amateur butler to our wild and now-infamous bohemian Holland Park Parties in the 1970s. Tino would dart like Puck, showering delights on all who came his way. Though a mere lad, he was brilliant. Assuring me, the Hostess (his senior by many decades), that everyone would be supplied with all they needed and, more importantly, even if it did not exist or had run out, Tino could convince the guest that his substitution was exactly what they wanted. He would exchange a requested whiskey for a Bellini with sleight of hand, accompanied by that endearing smile and look of confidence. This uncanny instinct was his talent in embryo. This abundant "talent" to criss-cross many forms of artistic endeavors could have been used by Tino in any career he wished. He chose to be an interior decorator. In some ways, it was the hardest furrow to plough, in that you are not free like a painter, composer, or writer. Working within the constraints of the clients—their sensitivities and whims—they become your canvas and paint. Nevertheless, Tino loves and embraces this challenge. With his ability to transpose his energy and imagination onto someone else, clients also find themselves creating, and the pleasure and excitement is reciprocal. Tino achieves this by having that odd mixture of being at the same time: Psychologist, Craftsman, Practitioner, Businessman, plus unerringly sensing what suits a particular place and often the hidden wishes for his clients. Giving them a home that they were unaware they wanted, but, once manifest, feels truly theirs. This empathetic approach and respect for his clients, as well as taste, belief, and commitment, is the secret to his phenomenal success. Tino's heritage is a combination of Alexandrian Greek and, on his mother's side, from Northern Ireland, my own land. He is a mixture of sunshine with a touch of the Orient and the more dour Northern Lands, with their long dark winters and melancholic shadows. This blood mixture with its myths and memories are much in Tino's nature. It gives him the breadth of vision and an understanding of the way other people think and live. Tino's company is an utter pleasure, whether looking at paintings, traveling to remote places, or working on a project with him, all of which I have done. He injects fun, laughter, and a sense of the ridiculous. Tino always gets the point and enters into the spirit of any undertaking with the same gentle understanding. Every moment of the day and night, he puts knowledge, sound, and color into a kaleidoscope—shaking it into different patterns, cramming his life with endless new concepts and sensations. Tino is one of those folk who scatter glitter, sparklers, and stars wherever they go. Lucky for us who know and love Tino, they are everywhere he is.

Lindy, Marchioness of Dufferin and Ava—Clandeboye, County Down, Ireland, September 2011

OPPOSITE *Twelve-year-old Tino and his twin sister Manuela were photographed in the back garden of the Zervudachi house in Holland Park, London, by Derry Moore. The famous English photographer would later introduce Tino to the interior decorator David Mlinaric.*

Foreword

When looking at the work of a designer and then assessing it, one has first to relate the appropriateness of the work to the period in which it was carried out. Then secondly, to recognise its quality: How well are its components made. These two considerations will be of more value in the long term than even styling, the third essential element, and the one that is so fugitive and which fades with familiarity. This is especially true, I believe, if the designer's work primarily concerns private houses. Tino Zervudachi's career covers a period of unprecedented prosperity in the western world. More people than ever before have been able to have houses fitted out to a standard previously only possible for a few. The large amount of work in design and decoration of people in his age group, both amateur and professional, expresses this, and his is particularly representative. The main danger of having too much prosperity, or too much money, is overstyling, extravagance, and too much show and emphasis on novelty. Innovation is important but it doesn't necessarily mean progress. Tino's work shows both a respect for the existing or the old and an enthusiasm for the new. It never crosses the threshold of excess and yet is glamorous and quietly luxurious. Tino was brought up in London and moved to Paris to start a branch of our design company, Mlinaric, Henry & Zervudachi, in 1991, when he was 27. He had joined the studio in London when he was 19. It was clear from the start both that the new venture would be successful and that he would enjoy it. As well as his visual gifts, he follows the traditional way of looking after a client, which is that practically nothing is too much trouble. He can identify what both the client and the building need or want very quickly. He has both patience and energy in equal measure. Going through the illustrations in this book, the reader will note at once how effortless his rooms look. Everything fits into place. Make no mistake though, they are very carefully planned. The photographing of rooms has become a profession in its own right since the middle of the twentieth century, parallel to the rise of interior design and decoration. Instead of attempting to show a complete room, first looking one way and then the other, as if doing a survey, photographers concentrate on the character or atmosphere of the place. This has affected the way rooms are designed and arranged. When looking at photographs of Tino's work, it is worth imagining the shell of the room without the contents to see his skill in putting it right in the context of scale, proportion, and the detail of the fitting out. Then to see how this is answered and added to by the choice and arrangement of the furniture and pictures. Usually one looks at the latter before the former, as these often look more eye catching. With the work shown in this book, both seem to me to be of equal strength, and achieve a harmony that one doesn't often find. But now as well as looking, read on. Natasha Fraser-Cavassoni's commentary is full of accurate observations, as can best be had from a contemporary of her subject.

David Mlinaric—Spargrove, Dorset, England, September 2011

OPPOSITE *This portrait of Tino in front of a photograph by Marianne Haas was taken in the Galerie Tino Zervudachi in the Jardins of the Palais-Royal in Paris.*

Introduction

In the world of interior design, Tino Zervudachi has become a byword for exclusive elegance. Traveling to sought-after exotic locations, Tino has created homes for high-powered billionaires, famous rock stars, and esteemed art collectors, many of whom insist on anonymity.

Recognized for his deceptively lived-in style and opining that "a room should feel effortless, and the proportions should work seamlessly together," Tino views interior design as a way of "creating comfort with the space that you have been given." He describes his main role as being an intermediary between his clients' dreams and the reality of achieving them. "Some clients can visualize what they want and others need to be guided," he explained. "The personal relationship is essential. It triggers everything else and creates trust."

Trust is a crucial factor in Tino's modus operandi. Clients rave about his taste, energy, enthusiasm, and how they always feel safe with him. This feeling cannot be underestimated and accounts for Tino's enviable list of clients, including some who have commissioned as many as fifteen projects, and others who would not dream of buying a new property without consulting him. Once involved with Tino, few stray elsewhere.

All of the designer's clients are impressed by his lack of ego. "Tino can think his way into a building without imposing his values," said Ivor Braka, the London-based art gallery owner who has known him since the 1980s. Melanie Munk, the wife of Peter Munk, who chose Tino for their vast project in Porto Montenegro, was impressed by "his passionate commitment to the 'perfect,'" his "multi-lingual sense of humor," and "his unique, endearing ability to make each client feel that they are the most important." Tino is adventurous yet practical. "I have learnt through him to go for the bigger picture and not to be so cautious," said Peter Simon, the retail entrepreneur who has hired him to decorate his houses all over Europe. Harry Lee, a Hong Kong-born patron of the opera world, appreciated Tino's insistence on superior craftsmen and general high standards. "As a result, our London home looks exactly the same as when we moved in ten years ago," he said.

Although popular and gregarious—"Tino is high on life," said Braka—the neat-featured and well-dressed Tino is discretion personified. Albeit extremely secretive about his clients, he also rarely talks about his family, content to say that his mother is Irish and his father is Greek. However, Tino comes from a wildly romantic lineage that evokes the heady days of pre-Nasser Egypt. Paul Draneht, Tino's great-great paternal grandfather, was a nineteenth-century Pasha. Renowned for his persuasive methods, not only was he involved in the negotiations for the Suez Canal, but he also convinced Giuseppe Verdi to compose a new work for its inauguration. *Aïda* was the resulting opera. Despina, Draneht's daughter, married Manoli, the son of Constantine Zervudachi, a land-owning Greek financier who was knighted for the promotion of British interests in Egypt, including Victoria College, the British public-style school in Alexandria. Despina and Manoli had five children. Their daughter Kathleen married the Greek Prime Minister while their second son, Laky, became a successful cotton merchant, in part no doubt due to the family-owned cotton fields. Laky and his wife Alice had two sons—the eldest was Nolly, Tino's father, and Marke, his uncle.

The Zervudachi family led a charmed, cosmopolitan existence. Their winters were spent in Alexandria. The week was split between their penthouse apartment that overlooked the *Guenana el Shalalat*, or Garden of Waterfalls, and was decorated by Maison Jansen, the legendary French design firm, and a beach house on the Mediterranean next to King Farouk's Montazah Palace. Summers were spent at Villa Draneht Pasha, the family's sumptuous mansion on Italy's Lake Maggiore, which had twenty bedroom suites, salons filled with valuable French furniture, and a fleet of liveried footmen. Twenty years later, an essence of the sumptuousness was captured by Peter Zervudachi, Tino's great uncle, when he opened Galerie du Lac in Vevey, Switzerland, an address which became fabled for its objets d'art and exceptional clients like Heini Thyssen, Gianni Agnelli, and international royalty like Empress Farah Diba. Being privy to an exclusive world from childhood gave Peter Zervudachi an inner confidence. As an antiques dealer, he made a lucrative livelihood from being driven by instinct as opposed to commercial considerations. To a certain extent, the equivalent could be said about Tino, even if the circumstances were quite different.

Tino and his twin sister Manuela Zervudachi—now a Paris-based sculptor—and his two older brothers were brought up in a sprawling house in Holland Park, a leafy neighborhood in London. Tino spent some of his holidays in Alexandria with his grandparents. One lasting memory was learning to drive, at the tender age of ten, "in the quiet palm-tree-lined parks" of the Montazah Palace. When visiting his father's cousin in Greece, Tino discovered the world of decoration magazines. "His American wife had them all," he said. "And I could sit for hours going through piles of interiors magazines." His passion for interior design had actually begun when he was four years old. "I was very interested by the opening and closing of drawers, for example, and how furniture was made generally, and I remember being very sensitive to the sensation of a cold stone floor versus a carpeted one," he recalled. Inside his bedside cupboard, Tino even organized a house for his teddy bear. "I used stamps for pictures on the wall and created a miniature world," he said.

Judicious beyond his years, Tino felt out of place amongst his own age group and preferred the company of adults. "After weekend lunches, I used to play backgammon with my parents' friends," he said. "I wanted to learn from them." Manuela recalled how attuned her twin was to paintings and objects. "From a really early age, Tino knew all the stories and where everything came from," she said. He was also financially savvy—"Tino's family nickname was TTT, short for Tino the Tiny Tycoon, because he always had some money-making scheme, like polishing stones, and making candles and selling them." His creativity extended to constantly rearranging the bedroom they shared, as well as framing a mirror with black tape taken from a cassette and deciding to whitewash a parquet floor in his bedroom and throwing a bright red carpet on top—"that was unusual for London in 1976," said Manuela. Tino would also trawl the antique stalls along Portobello Road looking for silver objects. "There are things that I chose then that I still admire and even surprise me," Tino said. Another favorite pastime was preparing candlelit dinners in the family's treehouse, which was "two floors and quite sophisticated," according to Manuela, in the large oak at the end of their garden. Aoife O'Brien, who was to become a future client of Tino's, happened to attend one of his parents' parties when everyone, in a united chorus, suddenly insisted that she see the treehouse. "I remember climbing up into this twinkly, magical hideaway and marveling at the enchanted atmosphere," she said.

In spite of his gift for interior decoration, Tino doubted it was a career for him until he met David Mlinaric, the highly esteemed London-based interior designer. Then, the nineteen-year-old Tino was assisting Derry Moore, the interiors photographer. "At a photo shoot in Eaton Square, without being told, Tino knew to turn the chair to be three-quarter, rather than the side view," said Mlinaric. "He just had that instinct." The next day, Mlinaric asked Moore's permission to hire Tino as his assistant. "I thought I would work for him for a year!" said Tino. The association lasted 25 years. Tino became a partner in 1987 and ultimately bought the company when Mlinaric retired in 2005.

In 1981, English interior design was fairly unsophisticated. For example, "complex lighting systems were only just being introduced," Tino recalled. Still, he was thrown into Mlinaric's elegant orbit, whose range of clients included Mick Jagger, Jacob Rothschild, and The National Trust. "David was my mentor and helped me to analyze space and to strip the information down,"

OPPOSITE *Tino with a new assistant, at the Paris branch of Mlinaric, Henry & Zervudachi, discusses plans, surrounded by images of projects pinned on the walls. The 1920s painting of London is by the British artist Herbert Davis Richter.*

OVERLEAF *A group of Tino's favorite objects stand on a one-of-a-kind cloisonné chest by the French designer André Dubreuil in his private office in Paris. They include a yellow vase by the French ceramicist Georges Jouve, a plaster lamp by Diego Giacometti, the Swiss sculptor and designer, and a ceramic cow by Rosa Ng Nguen, one of Tino's friends.*

Dancing Ledge
Derek Jarman

Tino said. "He also taught me to seek a logical conclusion. Sometimes you need to do something wrong because it works that way. That is what makes life easy—knowing what the solutions are." He was equally impressed by Mlinaric's rigorous sense of culture, his historical knowledge and his infallible eye. "David was hard on me, but patient," Tino recalled. "You have to be both in this business." Mlinaric, on the other hand, remembered that Tino was "instantly very good and hands-on. When we moved to our new studio, Tino got out a pair of pliers and immediately fixed the electricity, while his self-discipline and strength of character were ideally suited to the profession." "From the beginning," added Mlinaric, "he was always very attentive and polite with people, as well as fun. Mick [Jagger] and Tino were good together." Mlinaric also noted that Tino "could go into a shop or gallery and quickly pick out what was nice." "He's very resourceful at making it all work, regardless of others," and is incapable of creating "a bumpy ride," Mlinaric's term for throwing objects and styles together that bear little relation to each other. "Tino can always find the link when putting a medieval carving next to something contemporary," said Mlinaric.

It was an apprenticeship that grew to be professionally reciprocal. "Through Tino, I realized you could do things in a lighter way and not make it so detailed and complicated," Mlinaric said. "When he suggested shortcuts, they worked." However, by 1990, Tino was champing at the bit to open an office in Paris. In Mlinaric's estimation, it stemmed from Tino's need to "strike out on his own" and suit his more Continental than British sensibility. "By the time Tino left England, there were things that really exasperated him," said Mlinaric. "The British can be quite clumsy in a way that the Parisians are not."

Thanks to Tino's efforts, Mlinaric, Henry & Zervudachi found their new offices in Paris' historic and appealing Jardins du Palais-Royal, where the novelist Colette and the artist Jean Cocteau had once resided. "When David came to look at the place I had found, for the first time, he was grinning from ear to ear," said Tino. "And I remember him saying, 'This is world class.'" Tino transformed what was once a china shop by painting the walls, adding cornices, changing the floors to stone-and-oak parquet, and reconfiguring the lighting.

His first apartment was above the office, underneath one of the square's famous arcades that encircle the courtyard. "It had very low ceilings—but the detailing was still quite grand, though on a Lilliputian scale" Tino said. "But it was so lovely and atmospheric. Resembling another era, there was no sound of traffic, just people walking by or whispering late at night."

In Paris, Tino was immediately struck by "the high level of artisans, makers of trimmings, and other available details." "Moving there was equivalent to switching on the light in a dark room and finding like-minded people as interested in quality and finish as myself," he said. The attitude of the clients was also different. "At that time, very few English people were prepared to pay for craftsmanship, but "in Paris, I discovered a whole new clientele who knew what it entailed," he added.

Living in the City of Light marked the next phase in confirming the Tino Zervudachi style, which James Reginato, the editor at *Architectural Digest* and *Vanity Fair*, characterizes as putting together "dazzling mixtures of priceless eighteenth century furniture and pictures with the best objects and art of today, and making these interiors look like they have been there forever." Reginato adds: "Tino designs the world's grandest houses but the places never look showoff-y. They're loaded with style but as discreet as he is."

Just as Tino would refine his sense of contemporary luxury by being engaged by a different caliber of client and using outstanding artisans, what he called the "Parisian concept of perfection," which he described as having "rigor, with a specific place for every element," would leave an impression. In many ways, absorbing the 'rigor' on a daily basis and admiring the Directoire period and other architectural styles would further develop Tino's eye and help define his manner of working.

From 1991, Tino gathered together a team of artists and artisans that he still continues to work with. Though the range is eclectic—from the sculptor Philippe Anthonioz to the muralist Laurent Chwast—they all describe him as being supportive, knowledgeable, and open-minded. "Tino makes you feel that you are sharing something together," Anthonioz said. "Due to his attitude, you take a risk, which is great for your work." Manuela is impressed by his "fast decisions" and the precision behind his commissions. "It's as if it's already inscribed in his brain," she said. Chwast admires Tino's sixth sense for color and his urge to develop "new ideas around texture and effect." Chwast also appreciates how Tino remains down-to-earth. "Never pompous, he realizes that every element in decoration is important, however basic," he said. Marcel Zelmanovitch at the Paris-based Galerie Diurne, where he designs carpets with Tino, savors his broad range of culture, how he dares to mix styles, and has started certain trends. "In Paris, it's rare to find a decorator who can be classical and then original, and yet remain so aesthetically at ease," he said. Louis Benech, the famous Paris-based landscape designer, however, is touched by Tino's infinite social graces. "He's always easy to live with and adaptable to his clients, whatever the circumstance," he said. Whereas Miranda Brooks, the New York-based landscape designer, underlines Tino's stamina, which has had her "trailing behind him for many a site visit, speeding from Capri to Mykonos to St. Tropez." Brooks describes Tino as "trim in all that he does," ranging from his use of a tiny overnight bag when traveling, yet always looking immaculate, to his ability for turning "a cupboard into the perfect bathroom."

For each project that Tino describes as a journey and collaborative effort—"Tino listens and never dictates," offers one client—he feels a tremendous excitement. "I immerse myself totally in the client's world," he said. "They have my complete attention because, one, they deserve and are paying for it, and two, that's how I perform best." To achieve his layered, lived-in look, Tino begins by figuring out how the clients live. "It's all about the cloth you have been given to cut," he said. "For example, do they entertain or are they quite solitary? It's essential to understand their needs because the light, volume, and circulation of the home have to come from that lead."

Once that is established, he will work on the architecture of the space. According to Braka, Tino immediately knows "which walls to put in and how to make an awkward space really livable." Lee, on the other hand, admires his "amazing way with light" which can lead to a handsome wall having "no pictures." Peter Simon notes how swiftly the projects come together, due to Tino's persistence. He is persuasive but in a gentle way.

The second stage is customizing comfort for the client. Tino is reminded of wild animals. "What's comfortable to a lion isn't comfortable to a polar bear," he said. To his mind, "comfort" is not just about soft cushions and warm rooms, but, "depending on the client, it is also about more or less furniture, bigger or smaller rooms, and clutter or less clutter." Clients admire Tino's sense of proportion and scale, choice of fabrics, and how he fits furniture into the room. O'Brien, a London-based client, describes his work as being "all about the creation of an atmosphere, not just the sum of the room's components."

Tino strongly recommends using color. "It makes a statement, gives personality, and warms up a room," he said. He also believes in breaking rules. According to O'Brien, this can bring out a "surprisingly funky side." For the television room in her vacation house, Tino made shelves out of "the cheapest black metal ladders possible." On another occasion, he sent her photographs of a 1960s side table. Initially, she was horrified. "I said, 'It's bloody awful,' but Tino turned out to be right."

Braka commended Tino for his casual arrangement of objects. "I have a tendency to make my house too much of an AAA-grade museum, but Tino instinctively knows how to leaven the dough and mix it all in," he said. The gallery owner also describes the designer as teaching him "to see things as a whole," and not just "in isolation." Looking easy is essential to Tino, who "cannot bear complication in a room" and, in many ways, his work is a delicate balancing act of achieving the effortless, never losing sight of the overall vision, and dealing with the functional, detail-oriented side of his business, which he compares "to building an Eiffel Tower out of little pieces of matchsticks that are half-a-centimeter long."

Tino cites "patience, awareness, and curiosity" as his professional driving forces, not to mention "a general enthusiasm to enhance someone's life." Maybe his best description of himself is having "100 rooms in my head at the same time. They are all there, with every detail—the door handle, the cornices, the cushions—and I am always thinking about how to improve things."

Natasha Fraser-Cavassoni—Paris, November 2011

OPPOSITE *One of Tino's office bookcases is filled with what he describes as "things I like." Included is a small figure made by his eight-year-old nephew and an astrological chart that his staff commissioned for his 40th birthday. It marks the projects and places where he has worked. The small painting of deck chairs is by the British artist Emma Sargeant.*

FULL MOON
VAN GOGH
VASARELY 1
VASARELY 2
VASARELY 3
VASARELY 4
PICASSO
AUGUSTE RODIN
SONIA DELAUNAY
MATISSE
PIERRE SCHNEIDER
THE ENGLISH COUNTRY HOUSE
CHRISTIAN BERARD
Sargent
BRONZINO
ALEXANDRA EXTER
DUFY
Bradt Montenegro
BRAZIL
TOP 10 RIO DE JANEIRO
ENCYCLOPAEDIA OF ANTIQUES
THE LAND OF LEGENDS
MONTENEGRO
Late 18th & 19th Century Textiles
HERAKLES

A FAMILY'S CULTURAL HERITAGE

From the late 1920s until the mid-1950s, Tino's paternal grandparents led the cosmopolitan existence, as captured in The Alexandria Quartet, *English author Lawrence Durrell's classic series of novels. Their large apartment, on the illustrious Avenue de Belgique in Alexandria, Egypt, overlooked the* Guenana el Shalalat *or garden of waterfalls. The main salon was decorated by the Alexandria-based branch of Maison Jansen, the French decorating firm that is still revered today for its timelessly elegant style. Its international clientele ranged from Elsie de Wolfe, the famous American interior designer, to the Shah of Iran, to Jacqueline Kennedy, when she resided at the White House. When President Gamal Abdel Nasser came into power in 1956, Tino's grandparents decided, unusually, to stay in Egypt. However, to avoid having their belongings confiscated—Nasser would continue to launch a series of decrees about possessions—they wisely sent many of their furnishings and valuables to their two sons, who were living in Europe. Tino was never in this apartment, but fondly remembers the terrace of his grandparents' next apartment, where he and his twin sister, Manuela, used to chase a pet chameleon.*

ABOVE *In 1894, Tino's great-great-grandfather Paul Draneht Pasha was photographed with his wife, Adelaïda, and his daughter, Despina, who would marry Manoli Zervudachi, Tino's great-grandfather.*

RIGHT *In the mid-1930s, lunch was served on the terrace of the Zervudachi apartment in Alexandria. Alice Zervudachi, Tino's grandmother, far right, is seated in between Tino's father, Nolly, when he was a young boy, and the family tutor. Alice's husband, Laky, sits opposite her and in between the family's nanny and Marke, their younger son.*

OVERLEAF *Designed by the Alexandria-based branch of Maison Jansen, the salon was furnished with an overscale sofa and armchairs. Tino was brought up in London with these pieces as well as the eighteenth-century Venetian mirrors, which were in his parents' home in Holland Park. He inherited the sofa and has copied it for various projects.*

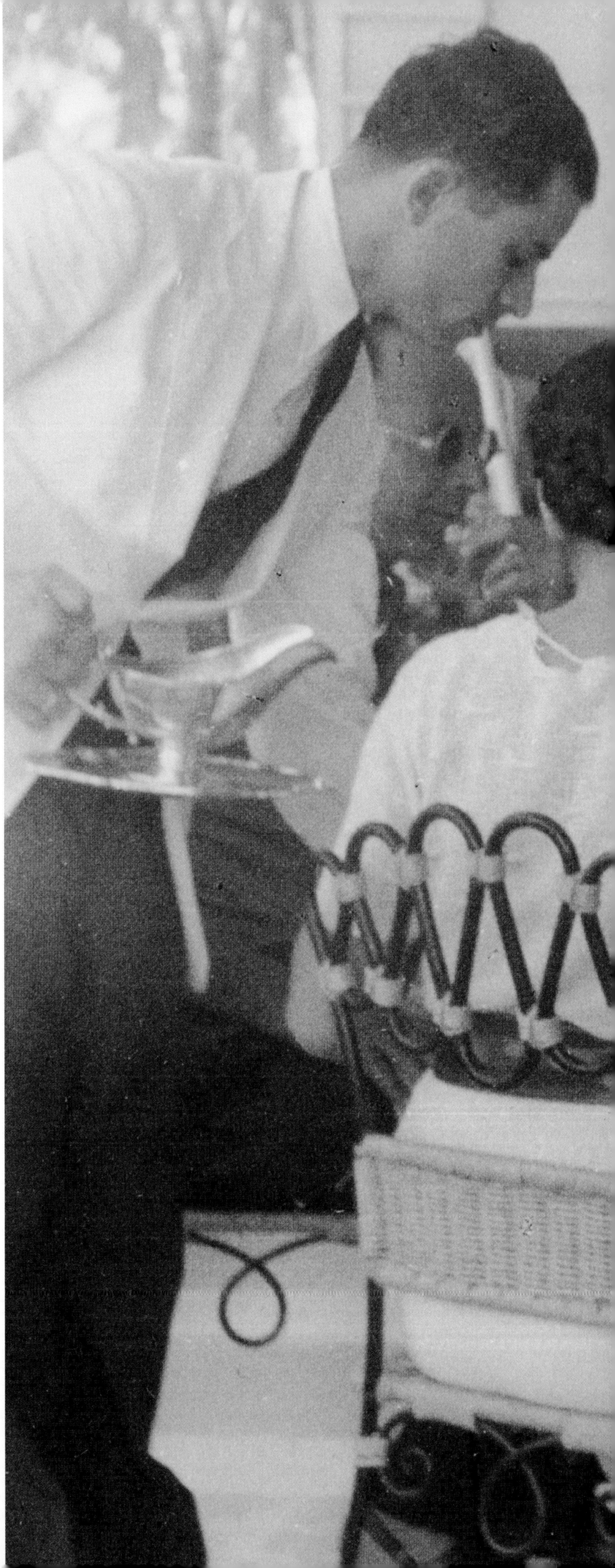

OVERLEAF LEFT *In the hallway of the Zervudachi residence in Alexandria, gilded baroque frames surround the draperies while an eighteenth-century Venetian mirror hangs above an eighteenth-century Italian console. Tino's grandparents were known for entertaining on a grand scale. Their spectacular Circus Ball—when Alice Zervudachi dressed up in a Marlene Dietrich-like ringleader outfit—was an international society event, and took place in the long, marble-floored hallway. In the 1960s, Tino's parents had the ornate mirror in their house in the South of France before giving it to their middle son.*

OVERLEAF RIGHT *Tino created an Oriental atmosphere in the dressing room of his apartment on the Rue des Beaux Arts in Paris. It was the designer's third residence in that city, which was Directoire in style. In spite of its being chopped up by the former owner, Tino restored it to its simple, elegant proportions, as well as its original parquet floors—by painting the walls parchment white, marrying an enlarged nineteenth-century photograph of a fellaheen, an Egyptian peasant woman, with a chandelier from a Neapolitan opera house, a framed nineteenth-century photograph of a Roman architectural fragment, and a contemporary felt-covered table that he designed. Also included are photographic works by two of his friends: Adam Fuss, the British-born artist, and Don Freeman, the American photographer.*

PREVIOUS PAGES LEFT *Tino's grandparents' dining room in Alexandria typified the Maison Jansen style, with its soaring ceilings, indirect lighting, and stone floors. Key features included the Louis XVI chairs and table, and a white stucco console that was designed by Serge Roche, the firm's most sought-after decorative artist. To this day, Tino remains a fervent fan of Maison Jansen. "The sparseness and purity of the lines made the decoration so modern for its time," he said.*

PREVIOUS PAGES RIGHT *In his St. Germain apartment, Tino was disciplined by the low ceilings that kept his work more careful and controlled. He restored the parquet floor and mirrored the recesses in the library to open up the space and create a contrast of light and dark between the rooms. The sculpture over the door is by Manuela Zervudachi.*

LEFT *The entrance hall in Tino's St. Germain home, which was located in the 6th arrondissement, was decorated in a strong palette. Tino had the doors painted in a prune red and applied Directoire-style moldings painted grey, the walls were painted celadon green, and the stone-colored linen curtains were trimmed in black edging, which echoed the Turkish stone and Belgian Black stone floor. The light fixture was Directoire and the bronze deer is from a nineteenth-century cast of a sculpture from Pompeii. A nineteenth century plaster cast of an original sculpture in the Louvre Museum of the Egyptian pharaoh Ramses II, which was brought to Paris from Luxor by Napoleon, faces the living room.*

RIGHT *Tino created a congenial atmosphere in the study of his fourth home by grouping art pieces by Fuss on one side of the fireplace, and placing an easy chair in front of the bookcase, in which the television is hidden. The oval table is by Emile-Jacques Ruhlmann, the French Art Deco furniture designer.*

LEFT *In the low-ceilinged living room of his apartment in St. Germain, Tino had the ceiling painted with a huge orb to give the impression of greater height. The pair of low, armless banquettes that flank the original Directoire fireplace were designed for the space by Tino to give the space an informal feel. An elegant, moon-shaped 1950s Italian coffee table, of unusually low proportions, lends a contemporary feel to the seating group, and contrasts with the signed, eighteenth-century Louis XVI bergère, which has been covered in a deep raspberry-colored silk velvet. Two tables of similar design have been placed to either side of the fireplace to suit the different-sized walls. An arched opening, installed by Tino, leads to the gallery—an open, mirrored corridor in the library, which can also be seen through the double doors and that continues on into the breakfast room at the end of the enfilade.*

LEFT *The living room in Tino's apartment in Gstaad, Switzerland, is on the top floor of a new chalet, and has views of the mountains, the cow pastures, and the local trains that pass through. Tino turned the four-bedroom space into a large one-bedroom apartment with room to entertain, since his parents and many of his clients and friends lived nearby. He wanted it to feel loft-like, though it is set in a wood cabin. He achieved a related look by using low, comfortable wood furniture and textiles from Indonesia. The designer is particularly fond of the huge eighteenth-century gong that he found on a trip to Bali, Indonesia.*

RIGHT *In the salon of his apartment on the Rue des Beaux Arts, the Louis XVI chaise longue is covered in a Senegalese fabric. A photograph by American artists McDermott & McGough hangs above a bronze sculpture by Michael Ayrton, the English artist and writer. The carpet, designed by Tino, was inspired by the work of French artist Sonia Delaunay, and was made in Tibet by Galerie Diurne, a Paris-based firm revered for its tightly woven and vividly colored rugs.*

BELOW RIGHT *The drawing room of Tino's London apartment, which is located in the heart of Belgravia and looks out onto the street, has a feeling of calm, accentuated by its symmetry and gracious volume. Tino used neutral colors, and filled it with significant pieces of furniture. The eclectic mix includes a Collette mobile that was previously in Tino's Paris dining room, and now floats above a French nineteenth-century terracotta figure; a white resin sculpture by Manuela Zervudachi on the French 1940s Macassar ebony desk; a 1950s wing chair by Danish designer Fritz Henningsen; one of the Danish furniture designer Arne Jacobsen's iconic Egg chairs; a Jean Royère-inspired sofa, reinterpreted by Tino; and a custom-made carpet by Tai Ping. The orange silk pillows offer the only note of color.*

PREVIOUS PAGES *In Tino's living room in his Porto Montenegro apartment, a remarkable large-scale watercolor by contemporary British botanical artist Sarah Graham of a cicada has been hung over a sofa designed by Tino. The cushions are made from antique ethnic fabrics. In the foreground, two cane chairs by designer Marc Newson frame a lacquered table from the 1970s. The plate, by Jean Cocteau, graphically echoes the black-and-white motifs in the room. Two bronze cachepots by Manuela Zervudachi float on a pair of elegant glass and bronze coffee tables, and the floor is covered with bamboo mats bought in Indonesia.*

LEFT AND OPPOSITE *The staircase in Tino's current nineteenth-century apartment was designed by Louis-Charles de Rémusat. The designer decided to combine two separate apartments and to replace the former dining room with a large entrance hall. Having moved continuously over the past twenty years, Tino feels that he has experienced Paris in a way that has allowed him to experiment with his own homes for new ideas. To create a certain formality in the hallway, Tino placed a large nineteenth-century French mahogany table in the center, flanked the window with a pair of 1940s Jacob chairs, and placed the cement statue of a rabbit, created in 1987 by Andrea Branzi, in front of the window. The black border on the Egyptian cream-colored stone floor complements the pair of deer statues that came from his previous apartment.*

ABOVE *In the dressing room, Tino had the turn-of-the-century paneling painted in white and gray, and chose furniture, such as the painted Louis XVI chairs, for their clean, simple lines. The cast steel chest of drawers with gilded bronze moldings sets the tone in Tino's dressing room. Although done in the style of Louis XVI, it was designed in the 1940s by Daniel Pasgrimaud, the French interior decorator, for a château in the South of France. Both the stamped Georges Jacob armchair and the Louis XVI guéridon date from the eighteenth century.*

ABOVE *Tino acquired the fine early-nineteenth-century French gilt-bronze and officer's campaign bed from a 1998 sale of pieces that belonged to his great-uncle, Peter Zervudachi, the fabled owner of La Galerie du Lac in Vevey, Switzerland. The rosewood bedside table is Louis XVI, and the steel chest is part of a suite by Pasgrimaud. Above it hangs a painted photograph by Anselm Kiefer.*

ABOVE *The table, designed by the German-born Joseph Gengenbach, who was known as Canabas in the 1740s when he moved to Paris, and was noted for his exceptional work with mahogany, is covered with stacks of books and a vase of flowers. To the left of the fireplace is a photograph by the San Francisco-based artist Michael Light.*

ABOVE *Tino fitted a mirror above the mantelpiece to visually open up the room. The mobile is by Daniel Chadwick, the British-born sculptor recognized for his mechanical evocation of nature. On the table sits a silverplated sculpture of a tortoise by French artist François-Xavier Lalanne.*

RIGHT *In the second floor study, an eighteenth-century mahogany gateleg table by Canabas serves as a book- or drawing table. Between the windows hangs a silver daguerreotype by Fuss.*

1 Comfortable Living in Classical Rooms

Tino has carved a reputation for his seamless way of marrying classical architecture with his clients' lifestyles. He is more driven to humanizing a house and making it appear layered and lived in than striving for an accurate historical reconstruction. "I think people would shy away from me if they wanted a perfect French or English look," he said. Although always respectful of the architecture, he is not in awe of it. "I would never tamper with a façade unless it was necessary to improve it," he added. The residences in this chapter belong to well-traveled and sophisticated clients. Their locations and the range of their requirements were quite different, yet Tino employed the same modus operandi when preparing the shell of each home. Decisions about the light, volume, and circulation of the space have to come from understanding the needs of his clients. Tino views their relationship as a partnership and an ongoing dialogue more than as a consultation. "If the contact is fluid with the client, the project goes well," he said. If there's antagonism, it sometimes shows in the work. The partnerships come in many forms. "When clients see themselves as the creators, then I become the mediator to achieve their goals," he said. "When they have to be guided, we work more like a tennis match." Most of Tino's clients cite his heightened eye for architecture. In fact, Tino insists that collaboration is primordial and needs to be harmonious. Still, he has an architect's propensity for logic and order before beginning on the decoration and customizing the comfort. This built-in necessity takes every element into account and delivers his clients' dreams.

LEFT *A gouache by Hugh Henry of a drawing room in an hôtel particulier in Paris, seen on the following pages, shows the embroidered silk damask curtains and some of the furniture and lighting proposed to the client for the room.*

REVIVING A GRAND HOTEL PARTICULIER

When I discovered the eighteenth century hôtel particulier on Paris' Left Bank, it had gone through many renovations, and had been divided up into apartments. Little remained of its original interior structure, except for the stone façade, the windows, and the inlaid parquet floors, which all needed restoration. This gave me the freedom to gut the interiors. Working with Laurent Bourgois, a Paris-based French architect, I reinstated some elements of the traditional layout while adapting it to a more contemporary lifestyle. The goal was to make it feel like a family home, as opposed to an historical reconstruction, and to create interiors that looked as if they had aged over the years. I was more interested in the five-story house having a distinct personality than having it look too polished. The garden, by Louis Benech, the famous Paris-based French landscape designer, added an element of modernity. The project took three years to complete, including the selection of all the furniture and accessories. The ground floor, composed of formal reception rooms for entertaining, evokes traditional, old-world Paris. The idea was to give a feeling of elegant opulence as opposed to indulgent, over-the-top grandiosity. The fabrics for the curtains were custom-made, the carpets were specially woven, and the pieces of eighteenth- and nineteenth-century furniture were especially bought and re-upholstered and, in some cases, ornamented with embroidery. We used pale-colored fabrics to reflect the light, chose comfortable twentieth-century upholstered furniture, and, whenever possible, brought the view of the garden into the rooms that look out onto it.

OPPOSITE *The early eighteenth century hôtel particulier, originally known as the Hôtel Le Vayer, with its* pierre de taille *or limestone exterior, was commissioned by François Duret and reputedly designed by Robert de Cotte, one of Louis XIV's favorite architects. Before beginning work on the interiors, Tino spent many hours walking through the empty house in order to understand the light, and to visualize how the rooms would be decorated.*

TOP LEFT AND ABOVE LEFT *Tino chose Louis Benech to design the garden because of Benech's expertise in structuring exterior spaces. The garden was composed of a mixture of Golden Irish Yews, Summer Snowflakes, and Graham Stuart Thomas roses. The chairs are from Hervé Baume, and worked well with the specially-commissioned bronze table that was designed by Philippe Anthonioz, a Paris-based sculptor, who also created the bronze terrace lanterns and the bronze pavilions with copper roofs that flank the Sycamore maple tree that anchors the rear of the garden. Anthonioz is one of Tino's favorite artists. He admires his classic yet contemporary style.*

LEFT *The large early nineteenth-century library table and a hanging lantern set a classical French, yet warm and welcoming tone, in the beige-and-black–stone-floored entrance hall, which Tino had paneled in the Louis XVI style and painted grey.*

RIGHT *The drawing room on the ground floor encapsulates elegant opulence. Tino wanted the colors to be soft, "like a lion's pelt." He designed the draperies in a traditional French style. The eighteenth and nineteenth century furniture, the Louis XV fireplace in Ardennes grey marble, and the objets d'art were acquired from well-known Parisian antiques dealers, as well as established dealers from the French provinces and auction houses. All the fabrics, including the gold-colored damask of the draperies and walls, and the blue silk on the furniture, were specially woven by Paris-based fabric houses, including the Maison Georges Le Manach, an esteemed firm in Tours, France, weavers since 1829.*

LEFT *In the small library facing the garden, the walls were hung with dark green silk velvet. The bookcase, designed by Tino, which was made by Degroote & Mussy of mahogany with gilded bronze mounts, is a fine example of the high quality of Parisian craftsmanship.*

OPPOSITE *A newly made Indian Agra rug with a white background, made for the room by Beauvais Carpets in New York, lightens the floor of the dark library. Elegant Louis XVI chauffeuses flank the eighteenth-century marble fireplace bought for the room.*

ABOVE AND RIGHT *The spectacular dining room was one of Tino's most challenging rooms to decorate. He created the paneling with eighteenth-century antique mercury mirrors, and chose the chandelier and the Louis XVI-style table in Cuban mahogany. Tino commissioned the Parisian decorative artist Laurent Chwast to paint clouds on the ceiling. The Louis XV caned dining room armchairs were covered in a custom-made silk fabric from Le Manach and upholstered by Rémy Brazet. The mantelpiece is Louis XVI, and the giltwood sconces are nineteenth-century Italian. The Porcelaine de Paris vases on the mantelpiece came from the Galerie Golovanoff in Paris. Inspired by the romance and soft palette of the grand room, Tino set up an intimate corner with window seats, allowing the client to enjoy the view of the garden when dining in a smaller group.*

ABOVE *In the study Tino paired 1940s-style oak paneling with contemporary furniture. A desk designed by Tino stands by the window opposite an Eames chair. The lantern and sconces, by Philippe Anthonioz, bring texture and depth to the room. The remarkable collection of drawings, by Russian artist Natalia Goncharova, enhance the feeling of a collector's study.*

ABOVE AND ABOVE RIGHT *Bold Louis XVI mantelpieces anchor the salon and the adjoining family sitting room. Tino contrasted them with a custom-made iron-and-glass coffee table, a crystal chandelier, and twentieth-century accessories, such as the pair of French shell-shaped Serge Roche-inspired sconces.*

ABOVE *The library was one of the most intricate rooms for Tino to design. He wanted it to evoke Tolstoy's Russia—St. Petersburg as seen through a Parisian lens—and have a room lined with bookshelves. The designer had a deep-blue silk fabric especially dyed for the walls and had Chwast paint the paneling and doors in colors and motifs that pick up the details of the custom-embroidered curtains.*

ABOVE *A contemporary sculpture,* Yoko XII 2009, *by the British artist Don Brown, has been centered under the chandelier. Drawings by Natalia Goncharova, the early-twentieth-century Russian Constructivist artist, hang above and below a pair of wall sconces by French designer André Dubreuil.*

ABOVE *The doors of the library were painted by Chwast in colors that echo the Simon Peers embroidery of the custom-made Le Manach silk curtains. Peers, a British-born craftsman, works in Madagascar. The mirrored base of the console at the end of the hall reflects the floor, to give a sense of depth.*

LEFT *High ceilings, white-painted walls, white linen curtains embroidered by Jean-François Lesage in India, and Arabescato marble floors add to the serene, airy feeling of the master bathroom.*

RIGHT AND BELOW RIGHT *Since the guest bedrooms look out onto the garden, Tino decorated them in a more countrified style, mixing antique objets d'art, nineteenth-century lamps, and eighteenth-century pier mirrors between the windows. In both rooms, the curtains and the walls are covered in Le Manach and Braquenié printed toiles. The walls and beds were upholstered by Phelippeau in Paris.*

SCHUBERT

SOPHISTICATED BLEND IN LONDON

Built in the eighteenth century, and owned by the same family for over fifty years, the terraced four-story London house was in terrible condition when it was purchased by my client. The building had strict renovation regulations because of its registered historical importance, which caused this project to take three years to complete. We worked with the British architect Anthony Collett. He followed the layout of the four-story house that was fairly straightforward and typical for that era. The reception rooms were on the first two floors, though we turned what would have been small bedrooms on the top floor into the library and home office. The attic roof space was used to heighten the room. The music room, made from the former studio, overlooked the garden, which was designed by Miranda Brooks, the New York-based landscape designer and a friend of mine for 25 years. For the interior, I wanted to capture the essence of the eighteenth century and marry the client's European furniture collection with his Asian pieces, creating a sophisticated combination. My client and I were very much in agreement in terms of the overall aesthetic: He was always open to suggestions, was unafraid of taking risks, and thoroughly understood the design process and the precision needed to achieve the highest quality, allowing for the project to be truly collaborative.

OPPOSITE *A former artist's studio on the ground floor was transformed into a music room by reconstructing the skylight and enlarging the window to its original proportions in order to allow for a spectacular view of the garden, which was designed by Miranda Brooks. The bronze sculpture by the window is by Russian artist Dimitry Gerrman; the 1980s photograph of Louis XIV is by the Tunisian-born Gerald Incandela; and the lamp sculpture on the piano is by Anton Prinner, a Hungarian artist, and dates from the 1940s.*

ABOVE LEFT *To make the entrance hall of the eighteenth-century house feel restful and calm, Tino had Laurent Chwast spatter the walls to create a porphyry effect, which softly glimmer at night. The elegant furnishings include a 1930s French frosted-glass hanging lantern, a French 1940s mirror, and a nineteenth-century Chinese table in red lacquer.*

LEFT *Tino bought eighteenth-century Cordoba leather that he turned into paneling for the dining room. The unusual Louis XV chairs were covered with Lelièvre's royal-blue velvet gauffraged with a crocodile skin pattern and upholstered by Rémy Brazet. The curtain borders were designed by Tino to relate to the leather panels, and were embroidered by Lesage. The glass chandelier is a 1940s design by Bagues.*

RIGHT *In the upstairs drawing room, with paneling designed by Tino and faux painting by Chwast, the bespoke silk cushions and velvet-covered mahogany sofa, by Tino, mirror the colors of the Neoclassical early-nineteenth-century School of David French painting. The Chinese eighteenth-century chair is made of Huanghuali wood and is remarkable for its continuous horseshoe shape. The French gilded-bronze tables are from the 1930s.*

ABOVE *Tino created an elaborate round center seat for the drawing room, which is used mostly in the evening and for entertaining. The rare English crystal chandelier dates from the eighteenth century. The carpet was woven in Iran by the Parisian company Parsua.*

OPPOSITE *The green-glass mirror above the mantelpiece, as well as the swivel armchairs that echo the silhouette of the eighteenth-century Chinese chair, were designed by Tino and upholstered in apricot silk. The small bronze table is by Philippe Anthonioz. The neoclassical-inspired fireplace is contemporary and was made by Chesney's of London.*

RIGHT *For the combination library and study on the top floor, Tino designed a tall mahogany bookcase that was crafted in Paris by Degroote & Mussy and assembled on site. Books are also piled on an unusually wide English Regency writing table. The collection of vintage framed shells was found in the Pimlico area of London.*

NATURE'S METROPOLIS

ABOVE *In the hallway by the kitchen, a painting by John Coburn, acquired from the late Australian artist, is hung above a pair of eighteenth century Danish chairs. The striped carpet was designed by Tino and executed in Paris by Marcel Zelmanovitch at Galerie Diurne.*

ABOVE *For the master bedroom, the client wanted Tino to design a four-poster bed that had originally caught his eye in Tino's apartment when it was featured in* The World of Interiors *magazine. However, since the client was interested in elemental symbolism, he asked that this idea be lightly referred to in the bed's design. With this in mind, Tino crowned the four posts with bronze sculptures by Manuela Zervudachi, each representing one of the four classic Chinese elements—water, earth, wind, and fire. An English Regency breakfast table serves as a bedside table.*

OPPOSITE *Each of the door panels in the dressing room was designed to contain eighteenth century Chinese kesi scrolls. Extremely rare and valuable, each scroll was hand-painted with Chinese scholarly objects. The Chinese side chair dates from the Qing Dynasty, in the nineteenth century.*

MODERN ART IN A PARIS HOUSE

When a client wanted to move from a Paris pied-à-terre into a house that could accommodate his family, I combined two floors of a small Directoire hôtel particulier in the 7th arrondissement. The initial work meant constructing a staircase between the first and second floors, and expanding the space by creating access to the basement. Louis Benech helped make the lush large garden a key feature of the house. Its open views to other gardens give a great deal of light, rare in central Paris. My plan was to mitigate the severity of the early-nineteenth-century French architecture by demonstrating restraint with the styles of the doors and the moldings. Since the rooms faced north and south, and were pleasant to live in during both the summer and winter, I added new door openings and maintained the airiness of the bedrooms by using light paint colors and uncarpeted parquet floors, emphasizing the enfilades. I wanted to create an atmosphere of relaxed elegance to suit the client's bohemian nature, while incorporating his important collection of twentieth-century- and contemporary art. Placing such masterworks was not only a privilege for me, but also a true challenge, as finding the correct balance was essential. In order to do so, in the living room we hung the paintings informally, and offset them with a contemporary carpet, upholstered sofas, and pillows made from antique textiles. The house needed to suit my client when he was alone or when entertaining, so we made a salon just outside the master bedroom that could be completely closed off from the other bedrooms. Using my client's love of India for inspiration, we had the living room painted by Laurent Chwast to look like old, peeling paint, and the hall glazed and patinated a saffron color. The painted glass panels in the bathroom were inspired by nineteenth-century Moghul watercolors from Mysore, India.

OPPOSITE *To create a welcoming entrance hall, Tino commissioned Laurent Chwast to cover the walls in multiple coats of saffron yellow paint. The antique stone floor combines classic limestone and black Belgian granite. The oak staircase was designed to look as if it had always been part of the building. Tino had the wrought iron balustrade made by Dunod-Mallier; and Hartley's, the Paris-based company founded in 1844, made the stairway carpet. Tino purchased the nineteenth-century lantern for the client's previous apartment. Keen to contrast the old with the new, Tino hung a spectacular late-1990s painting by Beatriz Milhazes, the internationally known Brazilian artist, above a well-worn Louis XV sofa. Tino decided to retain the old original velvet and not to reupholster the piece.*

ABOVE LEFT Reflection of Two Worlds, *a 2004 clay and lacquered sculpture by Manuela Zervudachi, is near a nineteenth-century papier mâché urn, one of a pair whose imposing scale lends an exotic touch.*

OLYMPIA
RIEFENSTAHL

PREVIOUS PAGES White Canoe 1990-1991, *by Peter Doig, the renowned Scottish-born artist, and the client's favorite painting, dominates the drawing room. The eerily menacing scene is typical of Doig's work and was inspired by* Friday the 13th, *the horror film directed by Sean S. Cunningham in 1980. The textiles in the room were chosen in relation to the masterpiece. Tino designed the magnificent rug to look like spattered paint. It was woven in Nepal by Galerie Diurne. He had Chwast create a special crumbling paint effect for the walls. It took several layers of the powdery technique to achieve the look. The pillows on the sofa were made from textiles sourced from the Paris-based Jennifer Shorto and the Senegal-based designer Aïssa Dione. The lacquer-and-mahogany coffee table is a Maison Jansen design from the 1970s. Piet Mondrian's* Composition with Red, Blue and Yellow *dates from 1930, and hangs above a Louis XVI demilune cabinet. The bronze candelabra is by Manuela Zervudachi.*

LEFT *An elegantly-profiled armless banquette designed by Tino highlights the enfilade in the salon where one of a pair of vases painted by Antony Gormley stands in front of the Doig painting. The room looks onto a garden, designed by Louis Benech, that the owner wanted to be wild and rambling. To achieve this, the landscape designer planted flowers like Asian dogwood, new English roses, Japanese anemones, and "Sundance" Mexican orange blossoms, as well as shrubs such as Russian sage and lavender.*

RIGHT *A close-up view of Tino's use of textiles from Prelle, the illustrious Lyon-based company that began in 1752, illustrate the designer's way with color. The sofa was designed by Tino, inspired by couturier Coco Chanel's famous sofa in her apartment on the Rue Cambon, which had one long seat cushion. The small bureau is a French eighteenth-century piece. The contemporary piece of sculpture on the wall is by American artist Sherrie Levine.*

LEFT *In the salon, a 1945 still-life by Pablo Picasso has been hung above the nineteenth-century mantelpiece bought for the room from Andrée Macé in Paris.*

OPPOSITE *The drawing room leads through to the small salon where Fernand Léger's 1924* Le Siphon (The Siphon) *hangs on the mirror. The painting on the right, entitled* Composition, *is by Russian artist Liubov Sergeyevna Popova. Tino had the door moldings picked out in charcoal grey in the classical manner.*

ABOVE *The nineteenth-century oak paneling in the small salon was in place before the client moved into the apartment, though Tino rearranged the room and redesigned the fireplace with a plain architectural chimney frame to coordinate with the paneling, and placed a pair of contemporary uplights by French ceramicist Marius Fernandez on the mantelpiece. The Louis XV armchair came from the client's country château. The carpet was specially made by FBZ Bartholomeus.*

ABOVE *Tino designed the sofa so that the salon could function as a guest room. It was inspired by his grandparents' sofa in Alexandria, which he inherited from his parents. It was upholstered by Leinis in a cream velvet by Bruno Triplet. The pillows are made from antique textiles that came from both Shorto and Dione. The 1940s white-plaster vase uplight in the corner casts light onto the cloud-painted ceiling.*

OPPOSITE *By the window in the paneled salon, Tino placed a red leather standing lamp by Jacques Adnet by the sofa and next to a bronze guéridon by Manuela Zervudachi. The nineteenth-century Dutch armchair came from the client's château, pulls up to a Russian nineteenth-century desk, and faces the garden. The curtains, of Milas fabric from Vaughan Ltd., the London-based company, were made by Leinis. Tino designed an architectural trellis with a mirrored back to cover a dull brick wall outside. This element brings light and a new perspective into the room.*

PICASSO
& Things

ABOVE AND ABOVE RIGHT *Keen to capture his client's passion for India, Tino had French artist Florence Girette hand-paint Moghul-inspired Indian miniatures on the specially-made glass panels to cover the bathroom walls, using the elaborate technique of "verre églomisé," or reverse glass painting. The client was particularly pleased with the effect, which he referred to as being "an old Indian custom." "It is so rare to find such high craftsmanship in this day and age," he added. The curtains were made from embroidered fabric from Vaughan. The alabaster light fixture is from the nineteenth century and hung in the hall of a previous Paris apartment.*

ABOVE *To create the warm and cocooning feeling of the master bedroom, Tino wanted a burnt apricot color for the quilted bedcover and walling. The fabric was specially dyed for him by Antico Setificio, the Florence-based company. The curtains were made in a silk fabric by Rogers & Goffigon and bordered with silk velvet from Loro Piana's Interiors Collection. The twentieth-century lamps are by Just Andersen, the Danish designer reputed for his metal work. The framed nineteenth-century drawings of Russian opera costumes are by Léon Bakst.*

ABOVE *In the small salon overlooking the garden, Tino commissioned Chwast to paint the ceiling with yoga symbols. "It was an unusual idea that made all the difference to the room," said the client. Another superb Milhazes painting,* Leme, *which dates from 2002, hangs above a sofa designed by Tino, which has been upholstered in a cut-velvet fabric from the United States-based company Gray Watkins and covered with pillows made from antique textiles, which came sourced from Shorto. The nineteenth-century English leather-topped bench and twentieth-century armchair have been placed on a carpet specially made by Bartholomeus. The French windows open onto a large terrace which gives onto the garden.*

A SERENE MEWS HOUSE AND GARDEN

From the outside, the home appeared to be a typical small London mews house. However, since it was originally two separate houses, it was surprisingly spacious on the inside and well laid-out, with a light-filled long hall leading to an elegantly proportioned drawing room. Three sides at the back of the house faced a courtyard garden, unusual in London. My goal was to create a pied-à-terre in which a collection of nineteenth- and twentieth-century furniture and contemporary works of art could be arranged in a sophisticated and calm environment. In order to achieve this, I began by stripping away all of the previous decoration, which consisted of dark, heavy paneling and fabric-covered walls. It was also crucial to maximize the house's natural light: I had the walls of the master bedroom painted with a powder of mother-of-pearl to provide an iridescent glow; painted the salon and hallway a warm yellow; and covered the walls of the dining room with many layers of glaze, in order to create a texture that would catch the light. To compensate for the small windows, I designed curtains that would allow as much sunlight into the rooms as possible. The clients' art collection, and the furniture we bought, create a unique personality, and we added to this by commissioning pieces, such as a pair of bronze hands by Manuela Zervudachi, as an alternative to a handrail alongside the two steps leading up to the dining room. After major work, the courtyard at the back of the house was transformed into a tranquil retreat. François Goffinet, the Belgian landscape designer, made a beautiful space by enlarging the lightwell outside, reconstructing the flagged paving, and adding elegant railings.

OPPOSITE *An olive tree spreads its branches over the back façade of the house. The balconies were designed by François Goffinet and crafted in bronze by Joel Orgiazzi, a skilled French metalworker.*

ABOVE LEFT *A pair of French 1930s chairs covered in suede, and a small side table designed by Tino have been grouped by the bay window in the salon.*

ABOVE *In the drawing room, warm yellow walls and a carpet designed by Tino and woven by Galerie Diurne help maximize the room's natural light, while also creating a peaceful atmosphere. Tino paired contemporary works of art with comfortable furniture. A painting by a British artist that depicts a detail of a sandy beach with a concealed Sanskrit text message was commissioned by the client and hangs over a remarkable nineteenth-century Chinese altar table. The pillowed sofa is by Howard Chairs Limited. To the left of the fireplace is a white painting by Iranian artist Shirazeh Houshiary.*

ABOVE *The well-proportioned drawing room was spacious enough to offer a series of seating options. An eclectic mix of furniture includes a pair of Louis XVI armchairs covered in a red silk from Le Manach, with an unusual nineteenth-century mahogany occasional table, and a French 1940s gilded bronze coffee table by Ramsey. The two* With Winds *paintings that hang on either side of the door are by Lee U-Fan, a contemporary Korean artist.* Maiko, *a 2002 painting by Jason Martin, a young English artist, offers a dramatic jolt of color in the hall and hangs above a bronze console by early-twentieth-century French designer Jean-Charles Moreux.*

LEFT *Twelve coats of paint and glaze were used and then combed in order to achieve the warm apricot glow of the walls in the dining room. A suite of 1930s chairs attributed to Swedish designer Carl Malmsten and woodworker Carl Hörvik, with seats covered in a Rogers & Goffigon velvet, surround a table by Tino, which was inspired by a design by French Art Deco master Eugène Printz, and hand-made by Christian Mussy, of the Paris-based Degroote & Mussy. The carpet, also by Tino, was made by Bartholomeus FBZ BVBA in Belgium. The photograph* Saltworks #1 *is by Edward Burtynsky, the prize-winning Canadian photographer known for his images of industrial landscapes.*

OPPOSITE *The intimate study is accessed through the drawing room. A portrait of Marcel Proust sits atop a desk by Jean-Michel Frank. The leather chairs are also by the French 1930s and 1940s designer.*

OVERLEAF *Tino commissioned the bronze handrail piece called* The Helping Hands, *by Manuela Zervudachi, to lead up steps to the dining room. The work of art achieved with a patchwork of photographs is by a contemporary Indian artist.*

Fine Art and Elegant Furnishings

Over the years, Tino has garnered the trust of his many clients, many of whom own important art and furniture collections, by respecting their attachment to their belongings within the context of their personal environment. "Incorporating art into anyone's home has to feel uncomplicated," he said. "If you isolate the paintings or make too much of the objects, it can feel self-conscious and stop the room from working." Tino's main goal is to create harmony, wishing to avoid a stiff, museum-like atmosphere and to make the spaces feel lived-in. "There is nothing more comfortable than a room that looks as if it has always been that way," he added. The designer is also adamant that "a work of art is unique and stands on its own," whereas a room is the opposite, as "it combines many different elements and is a joint creation between the client and the designer." The owners of the following houses are passionate about their collections. However, nearly all of them asked Tino to place paintings and objects, and to help complete the rooms with appropriate pieces. "An interior is not just about matching curtains, carpets, and all the other stuff," he said. "Whatever is placed or hung should mean something. Otherwise, even the most amazing objects become meaningless." With regard to grouping paintings, Tino is not afraid of humanizing a great artist by mixing up different levels of their work. "If a room has three top Renoirs, it's less exciting than a room where the caliber of the Renoirs is varied but shows the different sides of the artist and his progress," he said. Tino is also prone to blending objects and furniture of different periods: "The contrasts," he said, "can be interesting." "Often, the weakness in one can amplify the strength in another," he added.

LEFT *The drawing evokes the warm and elegant atmosphere of the refined châlet, seen on the following pages, in which the daybed and eighteenth-century watercolors hanging above it are the focus of the dressing room.*

PATRICIAN CHALET LIVING

When clients acquired a pre-furnished and over-decorated Swiss châlet, they decided to live there for a year before changing anything. From the beginning, they encouraged me to stay with them as a guest, which was extremely helpful in understanding which rooms the sunlight entered and which rooms had the best views of the mountains. We worked on the plans for a year. Our goals included enlarging the house and the drawing room, and creating a dining room. I also had the idea of moving the master bedroom from the top of the house to the level of the garden and to construct an enfilade of rooms around it. The clients possessed a collection of Swiss Patrician Rhône Valley eighteenth-century furniture and very fine English eighteenth-century paintings. We decided to select the best of their belongings and marry them with fabrics that were specially woven in Lyon and Tours in France, bespoke trimmings, needlepoint pillows, and hand-embroidered curtains. The master bedroom ceiling was decorated by Laurent Chwast and his Parisian team of specialist painters. It was unusual to have that quality of furnishings and finishes in a châlet, so in order to avoid making it look too lavish, we chose warm colors and paid particular attention to refined details, for example, only local wildflowers were depicted, and the embroidered motifs were in keeping with the bucolic Alpine environment. I designed a partners' desk for the study with legs whose shape was inspired by a Swiss horn, and designed a coffee table-stool with a suede-upholstered top crafted from gunmetal to make it look rustic and as if it belonged to the space. Comfort was of primary concern to my clients. Three seating groups were created in the drawing room and the library was designed so that it could be closed off from the rest of the house. Due to its long design gestation, once we neared the end of the renovation, every element just seemed to fall into place. The project taught me that a substantial period of analysis can be very beneficial.

OPPOSITE *From every room, the châlet has sensational views of the snow-capped mountain landscape.*

ABOVE LEFT *Tino designed a series of sofas for the terrace. These incorporated chests that were designed to store the cushions. According to the owner, the chests' dimensions are so accurate that storing the cushions feels like "packing the back of a Ferrari."*

LEFT AND BELOW LEFT *As an example of Tino's attention to details, he had all the curtains bordered with embroidery, and had custom-made silk trimmings created to match. For the passementerie in the drawing room,* left, *red silk was applied to brown felt and superbly stitched by Jean-François Lesage in India. For the embroidery on the curtains in the library,* below left, *Tino used motifs with the Lesage workshop that were both refined and appropriate to the Alpine setting.*

OPPOSITE *In the summer, the furniture in the enlarged drawing room wears its light-colored slipcovers in order to achieve a feeling of understated luxury and coolness. Tino had the pillows covered in specially-made silk brocatelle from Prelle, and upholstered the Louis XV armchairs in a Toiles de Tours by Le Manach. Finding an interesting coffee table that would suit the rich fabrics and furniture, as well as the French limestone fireplace, became difficult, so Tino decided to commission Philippe Anthonioz to make a contemporary bronze table, since he feels that any Anthonioz furniture, though contemporary, fits elegantly and surprisingly well into a classical environment.*

ABOVE *The daybed in the dressing room was designed by Tino and made from two antique provincial fruitwood headboards. Eighteenth-century watercolors hang on a Le Manach fabric embroidered by Lesage.*

OPPOSITE *A collection of the client's Swiss Rhône Valley artifacts include a wooden sculpture of cows, a compass and spinning wheel, and an eighteenth-century Alpine painting.*

MOZART
Classical Music 101
BEETHOVEN
GUIDE
TENTH EDITION
EDITED BY THE EARL OF HAREWOOD
BOOK
THE GOOD OPERA GUIDE
DENIS FORMAN
EAST AND WEST
MARY
HUTCHINSON CONCISE ENCYCLOPEDIA
IN FULL COLOUR
LE NOUVEAU
Petit Robert
POWER & GLORY
THE HERMITAGE
Jacques Attali
Pascal
La Faïence

RIGHT *Tino wanted the dining room to be a harmonious backdrop for the client's possessions, such as a series of eighteenth-century Alpine watercolors and an exquisitely crafted seventeenth-century rock crystal sculpture of an ostrich. Since the pretzel-back chairs were not part of the same set, as Tino had found them at different times, they had to be adjusted so that their seats were all at the same height. Completely by chance, he happened upon the pretzel-shaped mantelpiece in Paris and bought it immediately, struck by its resemblance to the chairs.*

BOLD COLORS FOR A GOTHIC REVIVAL

In the mid-1980s, a large part of a nineteenth-century brick house in a famous London square was acquired by one of my clients, but had been awkwardly divided up. The first stage of this project was to restore the main part of the house, with its imposing staircase and adjoining rooms, and the second stage, many years later, to reinstate and create appropriate interiors for the owner's collection as the rest of the building became available. During the first phase, we achieved the atmosphere around the oak staircase by stripping it of the paint that was applied in the 1970s, to lighten the space, and re-coloring a custom-made wallpaper to relate to the strong architectural detailing of the staircase. Later, we also made a large kitchen and dining room out of what had been converted into a three-bedroom apartment. Since the client was a collector of British Arts and Crafts and Gothic Revival furniture, we decorated the rooms in these styles. In the huge kitchen, we designed the cabinetry in an Arts and Crafts style and chose antique textiles for the curtains. In the dining room, we installed a Gothic fireplace and some elements of stained-glass windows, and designed an elaborately molded ceiling. Since the house faced north, the rooms were dark, so we compensated for this by using bold color combinations throughout. Ten years later, when more of the house became available, I returned to complete the second phase of the project. The client's remarkable collection had grown to suit the expanded size of the house. Upstairs, we made an Arabian revival bathroom, as seen in Leighton House, a museum in London known for its Oriental collections. In other rooms, where the windows were large, the curtains, made of silk specially woven in France, became an important feature to evoke the romantic atmosphere of the late-nineteenth century. All told, it was a wonderful experience, as my client was so open-minded.

ABOVE LEFT *The nineteenth-century terracotta pillars were found by the client in a dumpster outside of London's Natural History Museum. Tino decided to use them as a triumphal archway between the hall and dining room. The nineteenth-century chandelier is English.*

OVERLEAF *To enhance the client's exceptional collection of nineteenth-century furnishings and twentieth-century paintings, Tino painted the dining room walls in mustard yellow, and chose claret for the color of the damask curtains. The silk trimmings were custom-made and the velvet pelmets have nineteenth-century embroidery applications. The windows were embellished with antique stained-glass inserts. Both the table and leather-covered chairs are by Augustus W.N. Pugin, the English-born architect who played a major role in England's Gothic Revival Movement.*

OPPOSITE *A pair of curtains made from antique woven fabric by William Morris, one of the masters of the English Arts and Crafts Movement, frame the view into the drawing room. The pea-green curtains are made of silk damask, and were specially woven by Prelle in Lyon, France, using a nineteenth-century Gothic-style document for inspiration. The carpet is a Ziegler Mahal, and dates from the turn of the century.*

LORD GRANT US LIGHT

LEFT *To enhance the staircase and its original oak banister, Tino used a wallpaper designed by Pugin–the original design can be seen today in the House of Commons and the House of Lords in the Parliament in London, which were designed in the 1830s. Tino had it remade by Coles in London inverting the color allocations for a lighter effect. The painting that depicts Christ appearing to Saint John is by Henry Fuseli, the famous Anglo-Swiss Romantic artist and poet.*

RIGHT *The curtains in the guest room were made from a fabric that was specially woven by Le Manach in Paris. An original piece of Morris fabric was used for the bedspread. Both the nineteenth-century dressing table and chairs are from the Godwin Design Studio.*

BELOW RIGHT *Tino designed the elaborate black-and-gold cupboard, inspired by the Scottish Christopher Dresser, another important member of the English Arts and Crafts Movement. The fireplace was designed by Tino to surround an original register grate by Dresser. The painting above the fireplace is by twentieth-century British artist L.S. Lowry.*

ABOVE *The curtains and headboard made from a silk damask originally designed by André Groult in the 1930s, the French Art Deco furniture designer, and made by Prelle in Lyon, was recolored by Tino from the original black-and-gold to this watery-green and beige, to go with the Christopher Voysey carpet. The bedspread was made from a nineteenth-century piece of crewelwork. The sofa is by Dresser.*

ABOVE *A Dresser cupboard and a pastel-colored rug by Voysey, the nineteenth-century English textile designer, complete the room. Tino designed the fireplace with ceramic tiles by William De Morgan, the English ceramicist.*

ABOVE *To create the Arabian Revival bathroom, Tino introduced a Moroccan screen and made the bathtub front from fragments of another bought from Christopher Gibbs, the noted London antiques dealer, and hung a nineteenth-century Tunisian tile panel bought at a country house sale.*

ABOVE AND OPPOSITE *Tino designed the large kitchen in keeping with the rest of the nineteenth-century feeling of the house. The cabinetry was designed in the Arts-and-Crafts style. The curtains are made from a Morris fabric. Leather-covered chairs by Pugin surround a nineteenth-century oak table.*

ABOVE *A pair of impressive oak doors lead into the dining room lobby. Four original ceramic plates by De Morgan are displayed above the doorway. The curved open shelves to the left and right of the upper kitchen cabinets were made this way because of their proximity to the windows.*

CLASSICAL AND ECLECTIC MIX

After living in a Directoire apartment for five years on Paris' Left Bank, I was thinking of selling it when clients dropped by who were searching for a pied-à-terre. They loved the generous L-shaped plan of the apartment, the low ceilings, and the many windows that faced all directions, though they wanted to change the feeling of the place. The apartment needed to suit their lifestyle and to house their collection of important contemporary and twentieth-century art, as well as their eighteenth-century French furniture. Inspired by their desires, I brought the apartment up a notch by making the drawing and dining rooms grander in scale; changing the existing doors for solid mahogany with ebonized moldings; painting decorative schemes on the ceilings to give them the illusion of extra height; and adding minimalist paneling throughout the rooms. The paneling was then crackle-lacquered white, creating a tranquil airiness, and highlighting their objects, which they enjoyed mixing together. Three years later, they acquired the duplex upstairs as well as the top floor, with its corridor and tiny maids' rooms. Once we finally received permission to gut the space, we made a connecting staircase and turned the apartment into a stylish house in the sky. I also made more room for their art collection by creating a large library where the River Seine can be glimpsed from its terrace.

OPPOSITE *Tino commissioned Manuela Zervudachi to sculpt a bronze balustrade for the staircase that he designed, which joins the three floors of the apartment. In the new stairhall, a 1960s urn by Finnish artist Kristina Riska contrasts with a Louis XVI iron vessel, exemplifying the wide range of the clients' collection.*

ABOVE LEFT *Reflected in the mirror at the end of the enfilade leading from the octagonal lobby and the library, there is an exceptional mahogany Louis XVI desk with ormolu mounts, and hanging above it, a graphically strong ink drawing by Pablo Picasso. These contrast with the 1940s Constructivist guéridon by the sofa, with its small sculptural lamp by Scarpa.*

RIGHT *A subtle crackled lacquer was applied to the paneling in the drawing room to give a faded and lived-in look. The treatment helped unite the mix of furnishings, such as the pair of eighteenth-century sconces that were hung on either side of a painting by James Brown, an American artist who lives between Paris and Oaxaca. Tino designed the pillow-covered sofa. The ink drawing on the left-hand wall is* Man in Green *by Pablo Picasso.*

Jean Després

RIGHT *Celadon green walls, parquet floors, and tall black-and-gold paneled bookcases give a dramatic look to the library. Made in Paris and glazed by Chwast, the cabinetry contrasts with the painting by French artists Nicolas Todd and Damien Fitch, and acts as a foil to the delicacy of the client's eighteenth-century Qing Dynasty porcelain pieces. Tino also made a focal point of the three-part Louis XV canapé by having it upholstered in three different silk velvets—a lighter almond green from Le Manach, a ruby red from Lelièvre, and a darker green from Edmond Petit—and placing it next to a Louis XV stool, which has been covered in a leopard skin fabric.*

CALATRAVA
Du côté des peintres

COLORFUL ART IN AN ALPINE SETTING

A few years ago, one of my clients purchased an unusual multi-floored châlet in the Swiss Alps. The 1950s house was very dark and poorly laid-out, with clumsy stairways and an impractical layout. It felt like a cramped cottage. The châlet had to be entirely reconstructed. Although complicated, the project was relatively easy to execute due to Swiss reliability. Working with Bruno Jori, a local architect, we enlarged nearly all of the windows to allow for more light, added an extra wing to create the master bedroom—which had wonderful views of the valley—and turned the 1960s-style shower rooms, with smoked glass doors, into four elegant bathrooms. I rearranged the spaces to be more comfortable and to accommodate the client's guests, but also made it possible for him to live on one floor when he was alone, in order to avoid constantly changing levels. I wanted to create a home for him that would incorporate his personality with his passion for art, making the châlet more traditional rather than modern and urban. So I changed the hobgoblin-like fireplace that was constructed from a strange stone column made of pebbles into a traditional plain plaster one with a wooden mantel shelf. We also hung the paintings next to the carved wooden architectural features that were commissioned locally. In order to ensure that every room had its own character, I selected simple furniture, strong colors, and sturdy, sometimes exotic, textiles that felt appropriate to the eclectic mix in this Alpine environment.

OPPOSITE *By grouping the colorful 1987 artworks by the German artist Günther Förg and marrying them with a carved wooden bench bought in Bali and a wooden archway, Tino created a châlet ambience that suited his art-collector client. The iron handrail was made by a local metalworker.*

ABOVE LEFT *To enhance the châlet's character, Tino wanted the wooden architectural elements to be a biscuit-brown color and to look dry and knotty. He achieved this by using local pine, and having it baked at an extremely high temperature. The pine floors, on the other hand, were treated with less heat and are therefore paler. Keen to create a rugged look, Tino rough-plastered the walls by adding sand to the paint. The artwork, entitled* Azulejoes (Hokusai) 2000 *is by Adriana Varejão, a Brazilian artist. The bench was bought in Indonesia.*

LEFT *Tino placed* Tempo de Verão, *a 1999 painting by Beatriz Milhazes, who is known for her joyful explosion of colors, at the top of the arched landing from the double-height living room to the combination sitting- and dining room, which gives a dramatic sense of arrival. Milhazes is one of the client's favorite artists—he started to collect her work well before she became known.*

BELOW LEFT *Tino found the dining room chairs at an auction. Originally painted white, he had them stripped down and then covered in a striped Senegalese fabric made of raffia and cotton.*

OPPOSITE *Inspired by* 100 Years Ago, *a 2001 etching by Peter Doig, Tino used cotton-linen horizontal-striped fabric with a similar color scheme for the curtains. The nineteenth-century wooden side table is French, and the ceramic lamp is from the 1960s.*

RIGHT *To personalize the master bedroom in the newly designed wing, Tino used a fabric for the walls that was inspired by Moghul-stylized trees and shrubs, referencing the client's strong connection to India. The painting above the fireplace is* Devolviendo Sueños, *a 2005 work by Spanish artist Juan Uslé.*

AVANT-GARDE ART HUNG WALL-TO-WALL

When I was asked to reconfigure the decoration of a large house in Southampton, New York, that belonged to an art collector, I had to completely rethink the reception rooms of the guest wing that had been previously designed by the late American interior designer Mark Hampton in a Provençal style. Without compromising comfort, I wanted the space to enhance the client's extraordinary art collection, which included installations and video art. Since the client liked to sit and admire the pieces, the rooms were set up for contemplation more than for conversation. It turned out to be a thought-provoking, interesting series of spaces. The rooms were very large, and there was a long hallway that linked the house to the new extension, which gave the sensation of being in an art gallery. In considering how to enhance the collection I thought to create a black-and-white theme, plastering the walls in white stucco and painting the wooden beams, woodwork, and floors black. To sharpen the living and dining room of the main house, the walls were plastered in bright yellow stucco, following the lead from the previous scheme, but giving the wall color more depth. The contrast with the bright white woodwork is refreshing. Apart from the bronze tables by Philippe Anthonioz, all the furniture was made to order in New York. Later on, I added custom-made rugs that were inspired by American artist Brice Marden's line drawings to bring a playfulness and warmth to the rooms. For the double-height room with the staircase, I designed a rug that was inspired by one of the client's paintings by Ugo Rondinone, a contemporary Swiss-born artist. We worked with a lighting designer to keep the fixtures and lighting effects as unobtrusive as possible. As there was little surface decoration, every element had to be executed flawlessly. The art collection as a whole forced me to keep an open mind, and encouraged me to find different ways to work with it.

OPPOSITE *In the main dining room, the table and chairs were bought in New York. The large black painting by Christopher Wool, the American artist, is balanced with a red counterpart on the other side of the doorway to the living room. Tino's Brice Marden-inspired carpets were made by Galerie Diurne in Paris.*

ABOVE LEFT *On the other side of the dining room hang* Untitled 2006, *by Josh Smith, and* Untitled 2000, *by Wool.*

ABOVE *The 1998 watercolors on the wall of the adjacent living room are by the Nigerian-born artist Chris Ofili, who won Britain's prestigious Turner Prize in 1998. In the adjacent dining room, Mark Bradford's* Starin' Through my Rearview, 2006, *hangs above the fireplace, next to Wool's* Untitled 2000, *a screen that hides the door to the pantry.*

OPPOSITE *The cast plaster ceiling in the dining room was created by Virgil Marti, the Philadelphia-based American artist. From a distance, the decoration looks classical, but as one gets up close one sees the details and realizes that the piece is made from casts of bones and skulls.*

OVERLEAF *The contemporary art collection, focused on prominent African-American artists and emerging talent from India and China, was constantly changing. Pieces, from the left, include a 2006 painting by Dirk Skreber, the German-born artist; 2003* Flowers *by Enoc Perez, the Puerto Rican-born artist; 2002* Radiate *by Michael Raedecker, the Dutch artist; and two works—*Honor Amongst Thieves, 2007, *and* It Doesn't Matter, 2000, *by Moshekwa Langa, the South African artist whose work is inspired by Apartheid. The heart-shaped installation on the coffee table is by Katharina Fritsch, the German-born artist.*

LAST LION
Damien Hirst

ABOVE *A pair of paintings—*Veil, 2002, *and* Poem, 2003, *by Shirazeh Houshiary, the Iranian-born artist—hang side-by-side in the entrance hall of the main house. The installation on the floor is by Cuban-American artist Jorge Pardo and dates from 2004. A 2000 painting by Ugo Rondinone is eye-catching on the back wall.* Childhood, 2006, *by Guo Hongwei, the Chinese artist, has been hung on the stairwell.*

ABOVE Slow Motion 4,5,6, *a 2008 series of paintings by Philippe Decrauzat, the Swiss-born artist, line the gallery-like hallway.* Shadow Procession, *1999, sculptures by William Kentridge, stand on shelves. The famous South African artist's 2000* Porter *anchors the far wall. With the help of New York architect Charles T. Young, Tino designed this space to connect the new wing to the original part of the house, and began the black-and-white theme with the checkerboard rug made by Stark Carpet in Guatemala.*

RIGHT *In the double-height-ceilinged living room of the new addition to the house, two works by Wool—one, 30 images,* Untitled, 1989, *the other,* Untitled, P254, 1997, *by Wool, and* Monument, Stalagmite, Pink, *2005, by the hip German-born artist Sterling Ruby, are dramatically displayed. Tino designed the circular target-like carpet inspired by the target-like painting in the hall by Rondinone. It was made by Galerie Diurne. All the woodwork was painted black and white as an answer to the installation of the contemporary art.*

OPPOSITE *A 2004 colorful resin chandelier by Marti hangs in the double-story space.* Rorschach test # 3, *a painting by Cosima von Bonin, the German-born artist, is above the sofa designed by Tino and made in New York by De Angelis. The bronze tables are by Philippe Anthonioz.*

RIGHT *On the second floor,* Decide Who You Are, *a series of photographs by Adrian Piper, the provocative African-American artist, and an overscale sculpture by Tony Oursler, the American artist, emphasize the black-and-white color scheme of the space.*

LEFT *Tino conceived the paintwork in the kitchen to echo the black-and-white theme of the guest house, including the blinds, with their alternating black-and-white slats.*

OPPOSITE *A 1998 stencil by Kara Walker, the African-American artist known for her black cut-paper work and grotesque depictions of racial abuse, is the focus in the dining room of the house extension.*

OLD MASTERS, UP-AND-COMING NAMES

After living in a Classical house, my client bought three floors in a former art school, which gave us the liberty to do what we wanted with the space. He wanted his new home to be very contemporary and incorporate his impressive art collection, while also taking advantage of modern technological luxuries. A known leader in the museum and arts world, he gave me a list of rooms he needed and together with the architect, we designed the layouts to suit his needs—the top floor was reserved for a master bedroom, dressing room, and an office for the secretary, while the ground floor included a library, a study, the kitchen, and a vast entertainment area that was further divided into a combination drawing-and-dining room. The project was inspired by his exciting and eclectic collection that contrasted new names with old masters. To enliven the windowless basement, we laid vibrant red linoleum on the floor. In order to deal with the lighting of the large drawing room, we made slots in the ceiling that can give different lighting effects, used illuminated tables to provide light at a low level, and graduated the sea-green color of the walls to reflect the natural light. Since the building had few windows and was dark, we used a lot of glass or transparent objects. My client had at one point thought to get rid of the family antiques in order to suit the new interior. Fortunately, we decided to keep the best pieces, which look marvelous in the contemporary setting.

OPPOSITE *The staircase designed with Timothy Hatton was lighted to fit in with the apartment's play between opacity and transparency. Instead of curtains, Tino chose to use Roman Shades with fabric custom-made by Bernard Thorp, a London-based fabric house. The 1930s French armchairs were bought in Paris.*

ABOVE RIGHT *One of the important requirements was to have a library that housed a large number of art reference books. In this dark hallway, the plaster shelves are backlit to give the impression of natural light coming in from behind.*

OVERLEAF *In the kitchen, the cabinets were painted a shiny lacquer, in a color inspired by the astonishingly dark grey-green of the library at New College, Oxford. The plainness of the seamless white resin floors and the Knoll table balance the strength of the color, as do the multi-colored leather chairs with chrome frames. The floating shelves between the windows for cookbooks add an airy and contemporary feel.*

NEEDLEWORK

ABOVE *In the powder room, Tino had a specially designed Japanese wallpaper made to contrast with the varnished ashwood door. The bronze door hardware is by Manuela Zervudachi.*

ABOVE *To make a feature of the landing, Tino asked Ingo Maurer, the prize-winning German lighting designer, to create a glass balustrade embedded with his tiny signature lights and a golden suspended ceiling.*

ABOVE *The master bathroom was a collaboration between the designer and the architect. A two-way mirror hides the television, the floor is of white resin, and the walls were imagined by Tino, and covered with "verre églomisé," painted by Chwast to resemble rippling water.*

ABOVE *The elevator, a moving artwork, was designed to include a digital art piece by Jennifer Steinkamp, a London-based video artist. Stepping inside is a fantastic experience.*

RIGHT *Although the apartment's main entrance is on the ground floor, the owner usually enters through the basement, since it is connected to the garage. So Tino chose to sharpen the hallway with fire engine red linoleum, hung a group of etchings by French master Henri de Toulouse-Lautrec, and commissioned McCollin Bryan to create a dramatic pair of circular mirrors to visually enlarge the space. The polished concrete console tables are also by McCollin Bryan.*

3

Calm Comfort with a Mediterranean Backdrop

During Tino's formative years, he spent much of his holidays in the Mediterranean region. Staying at the homes of his Greek cousins or friends of his parents and his grandparents in Alexandria, he soaked up a cosmopolitan lifestyle set against the backdrop of sea and sun. Places to eat pistachio nuts and other *mezédes*, and to watch the stars at night, became second nature to him. "Psychologically, I have always felt very connected to the Mediterranean," said Tino. Both his passion for the area and his built-in knowledge would stand him in great stead for decorating a growing number of residences in such sought-after resort locations in Italy, Spain, Greece, and France—including Capri, Ibiza, Mykonos, and St. Tropez. When beginning a project in the Mediterranean, Tino's main aim is to create a cool and airy atmosphere. At ease in the heat, he prepares himself by walking around the location and observing the way the light, shade, and wind change over the course of the day. As shown in the following houses, Tino believes in maximizing views and creating the home's harmony by linking the outdoors with the interiors. He proves that disciplined simplicity becomes sophisticated when a flow between the rooms is encouraged, floors are left smooth, colors are pared down, local artisans and their diverse talents are put to use, and furniture is kept spare. "The overall idea is that you cannot imagine the houses being any other way," he said.

LEFT *In a drawing of a Greek living room, seen on the following pages, the reuse of some of the owner's furniture and art from their previous house, mixed with new things, hints at the surprising and enjoyable process that brought new life to old friends.*

COOLNESS AND CALM IN GREECE

In an exceptionally green and unspoilt part of the Greek mainland, I was asked to help a small house that had become available next to a client's parents' property come to life, and become a simple and elegant modern home. Since I had previously worked with this client, I already knew her taste, and instead of hiring an architect, we decided that it would be easier for me to design the house myself. The first phase included turning a pokey, dark 1960s structure with an old-fashioned and over-planted garden into an airy, serene home that would complement its ravishing location. During the second phase, I built a new wing with a number of guest bedrooms, each of which had its own terrace. Although traditional in construction, the ambiance had to feel authentically Greek—and modern—with spacious rooms and shady places to sit. A feeling of tranquility was achieved by bringing the garden and terraces into the rooms. To lighten the interiors, I had the walls painted white and the beams and woodwork painted, for the most part, in blue, as an antidote to the summer heat, which also suited the client's wish for the house to feel classical and minimal. I wanted to keep the rooms uncluttered and I mostly used furniture that was custom-made, some of it locally, as well as some pieces that came from my client's previous house in another part of Greece. It is essentially a vacation house, occupied at Easter and in the summertime when she and her children and friends spend most of their time outside on the terraces or in the courtyard, so I designed an arch to sit under as a protection from the wind, and kept the main living space as a room to circulate through to the rest of the house.

OPPOSITE *For the high-ceilinged main living space, Tino persuaded the client to use a sofa and armchairs by T.H. Robsjohn-Gibbings, the British architect, that had once belonged to her grandmother. "Tino has incredible instincts when bringing in the old with the new," said the client. The 1995 blue painting,* A Dream of Reason, *is by the British artist Victor Pasmore.*

ABOVE LEFT *The inner courtyard was paved in local stone and the table was designed by Tino to fit into an arched niche for eating or resting. The traditional Greek chair gives an authentic feeling.*

OVERLEAF *Tino used traditional Greek paving stones, known as* plakakia, *to give the villa's terraces an authentic look. Furniture by the late American designer Michael Taylor, whose firm was based in San Francisco, California, large terracotta urns, and a reshaping of the garden helped transform it into a lush Mediterranean hideout.*

RIGHT *To give a sense of seaside lightness to the main living space, Tino had the walls painted white and the heavy wood beams a pale grey-blue. He created smooth floors by using large slabs of white Greek stone with no joints and then highly polished. The coffee table is by Christophe Delcourt, a modern French designer. The linen pillows were made in Turkey. The 1993 painting of a school of fish, entitled* Tweed Tyne Tees, *is by Julian Meredith, a Scottish-based artist known for his woodcuts, use of blue, and the fossil-like quality of his work. The large Turkish-style daybed by the fireplace was designed to foreshorten the length of the room and as a contemporary take on the traditional beds in old Greek houses of the Dodecanese. The plaster sconces in the shape of shells were designed by Tino and made by Manuela Zervudachi.*

LEFT *In the hallway of the new extension—"You would never know it had not always been there, and was another example of Tino's gift at joining the old with the new," said the client—Tino used locally made wood planks for the floors and ceilings, painted the floor putty white, and had curtains made out of a pinstripe linen fabric from the Paris-based Dominique Kieffer.*

RIGHT *In the newly designed wing, Tino created an enfilade between the study and the master bedroom that has a window with a view of the sea, and an adjoining bathroom.*

OPPOSITE *In one of the new guest rooms, Tino thought to keep a fresh and crisp atmosphere, covering a comfortable sofa in a blue-and-white Fortuny fabric, hanging a photograph by the contemporary Japan-born artist Hiroshi Sugimoto, and adding simple lamps in white plaster.*

ABOVE *Tino had the bathtub in a guest bathroom encased in sandblasted Greek limestone. The same stone was used to make a partition that hides the shower. The ceramic table was designed by Paris-based designers Mattia Bonetti and Elisabeth Garouste.*

ABOVE *In this walk-in shower, Tino used a dramatic black-and-white Greek marble called* Lefkada.

REFINED RESIDENCE IN THE SUN

For a very exacting and refined client, I was asked to create a home in a remarkable setting on which had previously stood a small seaside house right at the water's edge on a Greek island. The land had a small beach and wonderful sunset views. Working with the Greek architect Eva Mavrakis, we built a new house, which took 18 months from start to finish. In consideration of the strict building constraints—we were allowed to develop only a reduced amount of square meters. My rough sketch of the layout included a high-ceilinged drawing room, a study, a hallway, a master bedroom suite, and three guest rooms. Louis Benech created the gardens, including a Persian Garden. As my clients like to entertain in a refined, formal fashion, they were not looking for a carefree, casual vacation home but instead wanted a calm and sophisticated setting that would also suit their lifestyle, which included using the house in different seasons. The drawing room became the heart of the house because it had wonderful views—looking out to the sea in the front and opening onto the Persian Garden in the back. Since there were covered terraces on both sides, there was no direct sunlight coming through the large glass doors, so I had small windows installed high up to allow the light to stream into the room. Due to the limited space, the guest rooms had to be placed underneath the drawing room, and each of these rooms open onto a private terrace. I omitted a formal dining room and configured a number of different places to eat. We called on local craftsmen to paint the walls and to pave the floors in a pale beige stone. The project went very smoothly, and we were surpised at the standard of building that was able to be accomplished. This easy process can be felt in the quality of the finishes.

ABOVE AND RIGHT *Different seating areas on the terrace that overlooked the sea allowed for a variation in mood. Designer Marc Newson's zany wicker chairs contrasted with a high-legged Balinese sofa and a stocky armchair and ottoman from Michael Taylor. A cast-iron and teak Aladdin table, by the French designer Nicolas Aubagnac, and walnut-and-cane chairs from Flexform, which were upholstered in a DeLany & Long fabric, set a more formal tone for the breakfast area.*

ABOVE *The wide terrace was framed by fertile vegetation such as bougainvillea, African lilies, lemon trees, and blue plumbago, all imagined by Louis Benech. For this area of the terrace with outdoor furniture by the late California designer Michael Taylor, Tino planned with the owners to have a cool, shaded place to relax and watch the setting sun.*

ABOVE *The living room that offers a spectacular view of the sea is open to the Persian garden at the back, and at the front to the Mediterranean horizon. The idea of this living room was to have it feel like a covered outdoor space.*

OVERLEAF *In the drawing room, Tino injected a feeling of modern luxury by choosing mostly specially-designed European pieces. These included the chandelier by Christophe Pascaud, a French designer; the parchment and bleached-oak desk from Cicero Belgium; American architect Frank Gehry's Hat Trick chair from Knoll; a straw-framed mirror especially ordered from Lionel Sanderson in Paris; and a carpet designed by Tino that was woven by the Galerie Diurne. An enclosed terrace with Moroccan Moucharabieh-style lattice wood screens leads out to the Persian garden that includes a mix of jasmine and silk trees, and was designed by Benech to be both poetic and decorative. A ceramic sculpture by French artist Niki de Saint Phalle stands behind one of the low-backed sofas, from Ecart, covered in a Senegalese raffia fabric.*

LEFT *Tino kept the hallway that leads to the guest bedrooms uncluttered and understated. The walls were plastered by local craftsmen and the smooth painted wood floors are comfortable when people walk barefoot.*

OPPOSITE *In the living room, a bronze by Li Chen, a contemporary Taiwanese sculptor, sits in front of a painting by Alfred Reth, a Hungarian abstract artist.*

SOPHISTICATED LAID-BACK LIVING

When I first encountered the house, situated on the Spanish island of Ibiza, it was a combination of charmless and ill-conceived spaces, awkward bathrooms, and a cheaply constructed swimming pool. Yet, both my client and I saw potential in the isolated location, from which you could hear the sound of chickens from neighboring farms. It was also close to the sea, had a spectacular view of the town of Ibiza, and was only fifteen minutes from the airport. The building regulations were strict, but my idea was to open up the spaces to suit my client's relaxed lifestyle by adding different outdoor living areas and transforming the shabby guest house into comfortable bedrooms. I worked with Irishman Sandy Pratt, a notorious Ibiza inhabitant, who designed the garden and organized walking routes through the woods and gardens. Through the rearrangement of the spaces and structural work, we maximized light in the house, to create a relaxed environment, with numerous terraces on which my client and his family could do yoga, sunbathe, read, and enjoy the spectacular view. In the main house, I was careful not to change the footprint of the original building because of the strict regulations. However, by using local materials whenever possible, together we were able to raise the quality of the house, since it had to co-exist with the client's art collection and be appropriate to live in during the winter as well. We gave the walls a lustrous finish with polished plaster, designed fireplaces for the dining and drawing rooms, replaced all the doors with natural wood ones, used Moroccan tiles for the bathrooms, and selected good beds, thick rugs, and stylish furniture for the nine bedrooms. We made what had been a second-rate house into a really marvelous holiday home.

ABOVE *The stone-paved driveway, with planting in between, was designed to minimize the sense of a road through the vegetation. The avenue of cypress trees was planted by Sandy Pratt, an Irish-born garden designer who also ran his namesake bar on the island. Tino wanted the cypresses to be "tall and thin" to contrast with "the very horizontal lines of the house."*

RIGHT *The property was developed by Tino, working with the London-based architect David Connor on the initial concepts, and with Spanish architect Torres Torres on the construction.*

OPPOSITE *On the terrace outside the living room,* Between the Gulf of Paria and the Atlantic: Maracus, *a 2003 painting by Hurvin Anderson hangs above a table with a pair of Venetian glass hurricane shades for candles and a bamboo cloche.*

RIGHT *The terrace has an incredible view of Ibiza's landscape and town. "We made considerable changes to the terraces," said Tino. "But we were careful not to change the footprint of the house."*

BELOW RIGHT *In the new, atmospheric pool house, Tino used dark wood, windows with wooden shutters that open onto the garden, and installed a fireplace for barbecues. The standing lamp is Indian and was bought by the client on his travels. The tables were made locally, and the blown glass lantern is Italian.*

OVERLEAF *The covered terrace was part of the new addition and was created to function as a breakfast area. The furniture was made from natural materials, such as water hyacinth and even woven rattan, including the lampshades, to keep them from rotting or being blown over; instead, "the air passes through them," Tino said. The metal coffee table is by Yves Halard, the Paris-based designer.*

PREVIOUS PAGES *For the summer salon's color scheme, Tino opted for saffron, white, and oatmeal. The curtains are made of pineapple fiber, while the floor is of imported straw-colored French antique terra-cotta tiles that have Moroccan zellige borders. The armchairs were found in a Paris flea market and are upholstered in linen; the stools are from Ciancimino in London. The creased paper light fixtures were designed by the Italy-based company Taller Uno. Two paintings from 2002, made from wax and oil on wood, are by José María Sicilia, the renowned Spanish-born artist.*

LEFT *Keeping in with the relaxed, vacation ambiance of the home, a bamboo roof allows light to pass through and create a sun-dappled terrace. The concrete-based banquette has a mattress upholstered in traditional Spanish Mallorquina fabric. The brightly colored pillows are from Monsoon.*

RIGHT *Tino designed deep, buttoned, banquette-like beds that he covered with pillows made of a silk repp fabric from Sahco Hesslein. The black sconces are by Laurence Montano. The painting is* Red Flower, *by Sicilia.*

LEFT *The kitchen was designed with a Moroccan tile backsplash and teak cupboards with trellised fronts to give a slightly colonial feel.*

OPPOSITE *Tino designed the dining room and kitchen, added the elegant Moroccan tiled dado on either side of the fireplace, flanking the Portuguese nineteenth-century mirror with a pair of 2004 mixed-media-on-paper works by Miquel Barceló, one of Spain's most famous artists. The chairs, from Cèdre Rouge in Paris, have cushions upholstered in a fabric from Aïssa Dione. The custom-made chestnut wood table, distressed with marquetry inlay, is from Robert Grothier in London.*

LEFT *The staircase, composed of treads made from local stone, leads to the master bedroom. The balustrade and window frames are teak, while the seat with its sculpted bronze frame was made by Philippe Anthonioz. The mirror is Indian and was acquired by the client.*

RIGHT *On the landing outside the master bedroom, the tapestry depicting a cockerel is by Jean Lurçat, the late French artist known for his contemporary work in needlepoint. The lamp is by Thomas Boog, the Paris-based designer. The polished walls, one of Tino's signature effects, were achieved by mixing plaster with natural pigment and linseed oil. Referred to as Tadelakt, it is a traditionally Moroccan technique, which Tino describes as "giving a smooth, glossy finish that has depth and is cool to the touch."*

RIGHT *In the newly built master bedroom Tino wanted to give the sense that the room "had always been there." He used a dark wood ceiling, upholstered an Italian chair in an African textile, and covered the floor with a carpet by Allegra Hicks, the London-based designer. For the elaborate four-poster bed, Tino used natural and dyed abacá, a banana fiber from the Philippines, while the specially dyed-in-France Mousseline cotton netting for the bed hangings came from Simon Playle in London. The bed curtains are designed to serve, when closed, as mosquito nets.*

Master Suite
Main Salon

4

Collaborating with Architects, Artists, and Artisans

Although Tino describes his clients' requirements as the story that gives depth to his decoration, he regards artisans and artists as necessary components. "It's as if I am the film director, and they are the lead actors," he said. Whenever possible, Tino promotes craftsmanship to his clients because he believes that it adds "a poetic dimension, enhances the individuality of a room, and can turn the client's house itself into a work of art." When working in exotic places, he will seek out indigenous artists and artisans. "It makes the project look more authentic and tends to make the rooms more appropriate to their geographical and climatic location," he explained. Before starting the project, Tino submerges himself into the culture and architecture of the area. "If you arrive without knowledge, you are not going to understand what has built the craftsmens' creative ability throughout the years," he said. Since the owners were absent for the duration of the projects in Rio de Janeiro and Tokyo, Tino became close to the architects of these residences. As their rapport was very compatible, he was able to develop the interior decoration with the architecture. Tino had already worked with local artisans in Mykonos as well as with T.C.K.W., a Tokyo-based group of craftsmen, but Rio was an unknown entity for him. Thus, he studied Brazil's architectural history and became familiar with such icons as Roberto Burle Marx, the legendary landscape designer. However, it was the "attractive rawness and amazing potential" of Rio's local resources, as well as São Paulo's art and design community, that most inspired him. "I walked into this exciting new world, where nature is so omnipresent, and became thoroughly enamored," he said. "When working in a new place, it's all about absorbing the layers, and then letting your creativity interpret that."

LEFT *A drawing of the furniture plan for a house in Rio de Janeiro, seen on the following pages, shows the proposed seating areas and spatial rearrangements.*

LOCAL CRAFTS AND BRIGHT HUES

The glass house was designed in the 1980s by Claudio Bernardes, the esteemed Brazilian Modernist architect. Set in the jungle that overlooked the ocean just minutes from downtown Rio de Janeiro, it had been acquired sight unseen by my client and was in terrible condition. The previous family had used only the house's front terrace, ignoring the tropical forest at the back. Working with Luciano Pedrosa, the Rio-based architect, my plan was to highlight the astonishing landscape, bringing it into the interior. Bernardes' original concept was to make the house look light and easy, which he achieved by painting it all in white and by covering the roof with grass. However, once all of the furniture was removed, the house resembled a cold hospital with poor quality finishes and cheap concrete floors. To define the spaces better, I had the structural beams painted black and had raffia blinds installed to suggest a contemporary version of indigenous Brazilian architecture. This helped the house better integrate into its canopied jungle and made it feel less imposing. I reconfigured the interiors, placing the master bedroom further away from the living room terrace, rearranging the kitchen, and adding a breakfast room and bathrooms. After clearing a space at the back of the house in the jungle, I created a second dining terrace, allowing the owner to eat outside, away from the ocean. Initially, I worried about how to furnish the house, as importing into Brazil is complicated, and the client wanted the project to be completed within a year. Then I discovered the country's fantastic furniture designers, artisans, and artists, and decided to take a more native approach. For the color scheme, I tried to capture the bright hues of the landscape. I used as much wood as possible and limited the use of textiles, realizing they would only absorb the humidity and would subsequently become musty. I quickly fell in love with Brazilian design, admiring its harmony with nature.

OPPOSITE *Throughout the interiors of the house, Tino applied the bold colors associated with the bright green of the jungle, the bright reds and oranges of the flowers, and the brilliant blue of the ocean. To Claudio Bernardes' intricate glass roof, Tino added an element of shade with neutral, natural fiber fabrics that created a canopied loggia.*

ABOVE RIGHT *On the newly created terrace behind the dining area, Tino installed a fountain. The trickle of water mingles with the sound of tree frogs. Tino's decision to change Bernardes' white-painted structure to black horrified Luciano Pedrosa, as the new architect felt it was a sacrilege to the work of the original architect. Fortunately, Tino calmed Pedrosa down by showing him a book of Bernardes' work in which another structure had been treated in a similar way.*

OVERLEAF *Like the rest of the house, the living room was Tino's homage to Brazilian art and craftsmanship—mostly rooted in São Paulo—which ranged from Brazilian street artist Nunca's* Guerreiro Gritando *painting to the rustic printed textiles, the sofa by Afrânio Cunha, based on a design by Tino, and the striped cotton kilim that came from Kamy Tapetes.*

ABOVE *In the living room off the terrace, Tino created a welcoming, playful atmosphere. The black-and-white art piece, an axonometric depiction of a stairway, by Regina Silveira, a contemporary Brazilian artist, hangs over the staircase that leads to the bedrooms. All the cushions and wood tables were made locally. The lacquered low tables that look like shipping pallets are by Brazilian architect Guilherme Torres.*

ABOVE AND ABOVE RIGHT *For the dining room, Tino acquired an approximately 18-foot-long wood table. Tino had the chairs painted in tones of blue that went from dark to light. They were designed by Alain Blatché, a French designer who lives in São Paulo. The windows face the new dining patio and its fountain.*

ABOVE *An artwork of wooden letters, by Rubens Gerchman, a Brazilian artist, sits on the table. The glass-topped table on the back wall, with its base of crushed drink cans, is by Aurélio Martinez Flores. The photograph is by Alexandre Orion, a Brazilian graffiti artist.*

ABOVE *A number of works by Orion hang in the hallway that leads to the four guest rooms. An oval-shaped opalescent globe lamp is on the floor. Indirect cornice lighting and floor washers illuminate the polished Ipe floors.*

ABOVE *Taking advantage of exotic local materials, Tino used Ipe for all the bedroom doors. The cool white resin floors offer a contrast to the verdant nature outside.*

ABOVE *In the master bedroom, Tino designed the bed with a wooden headboard to avoid moisture-retaining upholstery. He also designed the console table on the far wall to reference the walking legs in the photograph by Orion.*

ABOVE *Tino was amazed by the high quality and wide selection of marble available in a marble yard near Rio. "I saw colors and types there that I had never seen before," he said. The designer used marble for the custom-made bathtub enclosure and walls of the shower.*

OPPOSITE *When creating the master bathroom outdoor shower, Tino chose Ipe wood. He envisioned the area as being private yet open to the vegetation, and having a stunning view of the ocean.*

OVERLEAF *Tino transformed the original swimming pool by retiling it in an Op Art style. It was inspired by the famous promenades of the Copacabana district in Rio de Janeiro, which were designed in 1971 by Roberto Burle Marx. By enlarging the terrace and simplifying the façade, Tino reinstated the surprising mirrored wall that reflects the ocean.*

HARMONIOUS FAMILY COMPOUND

For some family friends who acquired a piece of land in the middle of town on the island of Mykonos, Greece, I was challenged to create a simple and contemporary year-round family compound. The project would provide each of the clients' three children with their own separate houses, as well as comfortable accommodations for themselves and their guests. The client also wanted to present his collection of contemporary Greek art. To find the right architect, we organized a small competition, and we chose the Athens-based architect Theodore Zoumboulakis. The project entailed designing a mini-village, with a pool house and guest rooms, staff quarters, and a garage. It also had to maximize the view of the Aegean, and take the weather into account; specifically, the exposure to the terrible and exhausting Meltemi wind. The architect's concept included an elaborate arrangement of buildings around the existing retaining walls of the property. The process was easy, as Zoumboulakis and I shared the same vision. Organizing the steep and rocky landscape, however, was trickier. The site was incredible—stretching from the top of Mykonos town down to the heart of the village—but when we engaged Miranda Brooks, she faced many technical problems, including dealing with the Meltemi. The idea was to create an environment that was welcoming and unpretentious, and that would suit the lifestyle of its owners and their gregarious children. This was achieved by a tremendous amount of careful planning. The spaces had to look under-designed and yet feel contemporary. To ensure that the interior was polished but subdued, particular care was paid to the proportions of the locally sourced furniture, the choice of fabrics and curtains, and the use of plain concrete walls and wood and stone floors.

OPPOSITE *With the architect, Theodore Zoumboulakis, Tino wanted neither to recreate the former 1960s house, nor to make the structure modern for the sake of designing a "wow" house, as it would age too quickly. The new house had to look Greek, fit into the village environment, and be striking.*

ABOVE TOP RIGHT *Influenced by the view of the Mediterranean, Tino wanted the color of the swimming pool to be exactly the same color as the sea. After many attempts, dark grey paint produced the correct shade. The outdoor furniture is from Unopiù.*

ABOVE RIGHT *To suit the house's simple ambiance, Tino created a shaded area with bamboo and wood. The white stone-topped table was specially made by local artisans.*

OVERLEAF *Since the compound was on a hill, every area had a sensational view of the town of Mykonos. Tino described the project as "a walled village within the village," and allowed the designer to visit the island throughout the year whilst the project was developing. He described it as "delightful," since the town is "so overrun in the summer, yet deliciously quiet in the winter."*

REMEZZO

RIGHT *Being able to relax in the shade was an essential component of the house's design. The terrace, which is enclosed by rough stone walls to protect people from the wind, is an essential area of the house. It communicates directly with the living room and the views to the port, and is the principal space out of the sun and the wind in which to enjoy drinks and meals. Tino designed the built-in sofa of painted white cement, with cushions and throw pillows that were upholstered in outdoor fabrics from Pierre Frey.*

RIGHT *A serene simplicity reigns over the house, especially in the living room. Tino achieved this by using a minimum of color and being careful with the placement of the client's art collection. Framed photographs by the Greek artist Platon Rivellis hang on the painted cement walls, while the furniture is a mix of locally made items, low tables and pottery by the Greek artist Eleni Vernadaki, a Candide bench by Julie Prisca, and side tables that came from Axel Vervoordt, the Belgian antiques dealer. To unite the living room and the terrace, Tino used the same grey flooring of hand-hewn slabs referred to as* plakakia *in Greece. When the doors are open, both spaces appear to be continuous. The asymmetrical black iron fireplace hood was designed by Tino and Theodore Zoumboulakis to relate to the dining table.*

OPPOSITE *In the entrance hall, a photograph by French-born artist Jean-Baptiste Huynh, of a donkey—a familiar sight on many Greek islands—was hung above a nineteenth-century wooden Greek chest. The mirror above the staircase is from the gallery of Peggy Zoumboulakis.*

ABOVE *In the dining room of the main house, Tino and the owners wanted to achieve a feeling of uncluttered simplicity, even when they chose such sophisticated pieces as Liana Vassolou's metal dining room table with its asymmetrical single pedestal base that is fixed directly into the floor. The Arija cane and brown metal chairs are from Vittorio Bonacina. The delicate bronze olive tree sculpture is by Angelos Panayiotides. The lifesize donkey is by the Greek artist Vasiliki Perka. The mixed-media panel on the right is a 1976 work by Greek artist Costas Tsoclis.*

LEFT *The built-in bookcases, with their thick oak shelves, were made from local stone and incorporated into the staircase wall, which bisects the living room on a westerly axis.*

OPPOSITE *Since much of the activity of the property was centered around the swimming pool, the kitchen in the pool house had to be practical. It was designed as a long white cement counter that not only accommodated the stove but could also function as an outdoor bar, and stretches from inside the house to the outside on the lines of the retaining walls.*

LEFT *The guest rooms were kept light with white-lacquered light fixtures from Manufactor, and cast-iron curtain rods from Caravane.*

BELOW LEFT *Tino designed the master bedroom to be a calming space, with plain white-painted walls, and wide-plank painted wood floors. The curtains were made with Le Manach's blue-and-white striped linen. The red flower painting is by Panayiotis Tetsis, the Greek artist. The artwork above the bed is by the Greek artist Alekos Fassianos.*

OPPOSITE *In one of the guest bedrooms, the unadorned stone walls and whitewashed bamboo ceiling create a mix of textures, with the bed cover from Caravane.*

JAPANESE-STYLE REINTERPRETED

One of the most interesting projects I have had the opportunity to work on began when a client sent me to Tokyo to look at a shabby piece of land on top of a hill in the middle of the city and said: "Find me a great architect." He wanted an extraordinary statement house that would have the comforts of a European home yet feel Japanese. After a lot of research, I proposed Kengo Kuma—one of Japan's most prominent architects, whose aesthetic is to make structures disappear into the landscape. Wood/Berg, his name for the house, was his first private project for a European client in Tokyo. The client asked him to make the building as large as was allowed for its space, so he designed an adventurous origami-like seven-story house made of steel and clad in glass and wood, in keeping with the Japanese earthquake laws. Knowing the client's lifestyle, I planned the house with a formal entertaining area to be on the ground floor, to have a library on the second floor, guest rooms on the third floor, a private sitting and dining room on the fourth floor, and the master bedroom on the top floor. In order to suit the architecture, I furnished the house in a reinterpreted contemporary Japanese-European style. As furniture is not part of the country's culture, we designed and had the pieces made locally with T.C.K.W., a company whose artisans are known for their expertise in traditional Japanese crafts. The idea was to use color to warm up the house, and maintain a very masculine interior. Difficulties arose as we ended up with some oddly-shaped rooms—one guest room, in particular, is triangular, with sloping walls—and seemingly endless windows that each needed three sets of blinds, allowing for different ways to control light. The completed project is an astonishing and unique house, however, proof that a genuine collaboration between the architect and the designer can produce surprising results.

OPPOSITE *Although obtaining planning permission and digging the two-level basement took over two years, the interiors were finished in six months. The master bedroom, as seen from the roof, has sensational views and is secluded from the rest of the house. Tino's Japanese-inspired furnishings, which are prevalent throughout the interior, give the bedroom its luxurious but masculine atmosphere.*

ABOVE RIGHT *Kengo Kuma's wall of signature wood-louvered panels, designed to filter as well as mold light, accentuates the ground floor courtyard's tranquility. Tino created a Zen-like composition that consisted of a maple tree on a moss-covered island, as if it were floating in the shallow pool.*

OVERLEAF *Tino knew that obtaining planning permission would be pivotal to the project. Working with earthquake engineers was an entirely new experience for him. Tino describes the house as being a "high-tech, luxurious and surprising space, full of calm and comfort" since everything is operated electrically. The Wood/Berg house, named for its resemblance to a wooden iceberg, demonstrated Kuma's talent for geometric shapes, and his skillful use of natural materials. To avoid the building looking too large, the architect divided the tower volume on the south elevation and cut it at a diagonal. Tino was very direct with Kuma, and the famous architect enjoyed their open dialogue.*

OPPOSITE *Culturally, in Japan there is very little furniture in interiors. In modern interiors when pieces are needed, they usually order them from established contemporary European companies. Here, however, every piece in the calm and comfortable double-height living room was designed by Tino and his team, and custom-made in Japan by T.C.K.W.'s artisans. After seeing samples of the company's craftsmanship that ranged from lacquerwork to metal latticework, Tino would sketch a piece of furniture or an object. In the main living space, the large jar-style lamps were created by seven different potters, and the fabric for the lampshades was specially woven and dyed by a talented fabric colorist. On the terrace, the furniture is from Kenkoon, a Thai company, and has been upholstered in outdoor fabrics from Perennials.*

OPPOSITE *The dining room on the ground floor overlooks the front garden. A specially commissioned mobile by Hirotoshi Sawada, a contemporary Japanese sculptor, floats above the intentionally cracked wood table, which was made for Tino in Bali. The Jacob Kjaer-inspired leather armchairs are also his design, so that their arms fit under the thick top of the table.*

ABOVE *In the living room in the evening, tall screens can be rotated for privacy to conceal the dining table and create a serene Japanese atmosphere.*

OVERLEAF *The walls of the ground floor living room were covered with washi paper—traditional Japanese ricepaper panels made for wall coverings, and the carpet was designed by Tino to resemble Noguri, a traditional carved wood.*

ABOVE AND OPPOSITE *The style of the sitting-media room on the fourth floor and the Japanese-style dining area were a continuation of the East meets West approach: The chabudai, or low table, was raised on tatami mats, and the floors were polished cedar. Roll-down window blinds filter the light. There are three sets of blinds, giving options for sun, privacy, or black-out, depending on the use of the room. The specially made tableware was ordered to enhance the different colors of the room.*

LEFT AND BELOW LEFT
The Hinoki wood basin in both the guest bathroom and in the master bathroom demonstrate Kuma's mastery with wood.

RIGHT AND BELOW RIGHT *Tino wanted the master bedroom to be comfortable but majestic, like an eagle's nest.*

OVERLEAF *The 45-foot-long pool's mysterious lighting was achieved by Kuma with the input of Tino and his team. It consisted of concealed, recessed mood lighting in the ceiling and walls. All lamps were programmed for mood settings. Travertine Navona stone was used for the floors and walls. The blue color of the water was achieved with lighting in the sides of the pool. Other details include a pair of custom-made black-glass doors that graduate from opaque to transparent. All the teak and stainless steel furniture was designed by Kenkoon, the Thai-based company.*

Bold Styling for Simple and Elegant Luxury

Tino is committed to making his clients happy: "More than anything else, that's the reason why I do this job," he said. His clientele is comprised very often of male clients and includes a certain number who have asked him to decorate as many as fifteen of their properties. It is easy to understand why Tino's modus operandi would suit such powerbrokers. Apart from his obvious talents, Tino is efficient, decisive, and reliable. He can be trusted to be discreet, as well as to respect budgets and deadlines. Tino also possesses the wisdom to show his clients what he calls "small clouds of pleasure in the process" and then not bother them again until the project is completed. Knowing their world, he is well-aware of how a spare yet luxurious coziness is key. In the following apartments—three of which belong to the same bachelor—Tino's well-lit and comfortable interiors give his clients what they want, as they exude a feeling of calm. Sofas are warmed up with colored pillows, furnishings are eclectic, and rare textiles and custom-made carpets subtly accentuate the art. He is relentless about improving his spaces and anticipating potential problems. Both these characteristics are essential to Tino's design of masculine environments that boast the latest in technology and always seem to contain an element of surprise. As Tino explained: "For these kinds of rooms it is important to give a sense of fun to the contemporary side, but also to be practical."

LEFT *The drawing of the living room of a Swiss châlet, shown overleaf, combines a traditional use of wood designed in a more contemporary way. The slabs of stone used for the fireplace were dredged from the local river.*

RUSCHA
AUDREY HEPBURN
RUSCHA
RUSCHA
TIM WALKER PICTURES
DAVID LACHAPELLE

FIFTIES INFLUENCE AND RIVERBED ROCKS

This interesting project in a Swiss mountain village was carefully briefed by the owner, which enabled us to create the appropriate spaces from a bare canvas. The newly built châlet allowed us the freedom to divide the spaces as we wished. Since she and her husband had three sons and entertained often, the idea was to create a laid-back and relaxing apartment in the mountains that could be used year-round. We achieved this by designing a layout with a spacious living room, dining room, open-plan kitchen, four bedrooms, and a basement room for parties, movie watching, or playing computer games. While most châlets have tiny master bedrooms, I made this one large and comfortable. The style of the interior had to be in tune with the imaginative and open-minded owner who was more interested in capturing the feeling of an era or movie than having a typical châlet with the usual red and green alpine motifs. She cited the Flintstones as her chief inspiration, along with elements from her favorite 1950s and 1960s movies, such as Blake Edwards' classic, *The Party*. So I decided on a bold color scheme with white walls and black-slate floors and, choosing green—her favorite color and omnipresent in the surrounding landscape in the summer—for the curtains, upholstery and carpets. I sourced local rustic and natural materials that fit in with the theme; unpolished pine planks with wood knots for the ceilings; tree trunk-like walnut for the kitchen walls; and rocks that came from a nearby riverbed for the living room fireplace. Although we used a pair of Jean Royère-inspired sofas, the other furniture came from flea markets in Paris because I wanted the pieces to be one-of-a-kind to give the apartment as much personality as possible.

OPPOSITE *The Flintstones-style mantel-piece, the unvarnished Swiss Stone Pine walls, and the green bamboo-fiber carpeting from Tisca Tiara, a Swiss textile company, contribute to the warmth and unusual style of the living room design. The idea was that the apartment should be anti-contrived and humorous, said the client. That may explain how Tino contrasted rustic materials with such modern design pieces as the custom-made Pendulum mirror by McCollin Bryan, a photograph by Tierney Gearon, an America-born artist, and the 1950s puzzle-like coffee table by Pierre Chapo.*

ABOVE TOP LEFT *The Polaire sofas inspired by Jean Royère further the informal atmosphere. Nineteen-fifties finds from the Saint-Ouen flea market in Paris include an upholstered Italian chair and the pair of tables with plastic laminate tops. The photograph of a glacier is by the German artist Andreas Gursky.*

ABOVE LEFT *Green curtains frame the windows in the living room. Tino's placement of the dining area in the same space emphasized the apartment's relaxed and casual spirit.*

OVERLEAF *The terrace on the ground floor offers a magnificent view of the Videmanette mountain in winter. All the outdoor wooden furniture is from Manutti, a Belgian company.*

LEFT *Since the client likes to cook and entertain, Tino made sure that the kitchen not only looked spectacular but was practical. Striped walnut panels for the cupboards give a 1950s feel. The trunk-like walnut theme is continued with flamed Nero Assoluto granite tops, and Pillarguri slate floors.*

OPPOSITE *The long asymmetrical dining room table was custom-made in Indonesia. The metal chairs, originally from a factory, were loosely covered in whole sheepskins. Tino wanted to inject a lively note by having them resemble a group of sheep. "By avoiding clichés," added his client, "Tino gave personality to the place." The black hanging tin lamps came from a Paris flea market.*

ABOVE *To keep the master bedroom contemporary, the designer paired the large bed and a log sculpture by Lim Jihyun with flea market findings such as 1950s light fixtures and a mirror from Fontana Arte. Tino conceived the master bedroom as the perfect place to relax after a long day on the ski slopes.*

OPPOSITE *The black lacquer easy chair came from the Galerie de Blanchetti in Paris. A rough-hewn table, sourced by Antoine de Sigy, Tino's Paris business partner, was placed next to it.*

RELAXED HIGH-TECH LUXURY

Situated on the top floor of a nineteenth-century building, this Left Bank Paris apartment was a warren of 12 small rooms with an endless interior corridor. Bought by the client to be a pied-à-terre in which to relax and entertain, it was in squalid condition due to having been lived in by an impoverished elderly couple for fifty years, who then rented the rooms out to students for income. Working with Laurent Bourgois, my plan was to knock down all of the interior partition walls, and bring in daylight by removing the corridor, and make the apartment more spacious. The apartment had fantastic views of the Seine and the Musée d'Orsay and, once the corridor was gone, it became an apartment with windows that faced east, south, and west, with sunshine all day long. To unify the apartment, I used a simple color palette and covered the floors with the same carpet throughout. A contemporary luxurious edge was added with indirect lighting, invisible high-tech electronics that operated the curtains, blinds, and home theater. We designed ribbed wood doors, and marbled bathrooms. To make the large master bedroom more intimate, we put in a working fireplace and organized an elegant seating area around it. We planned for the client's second dressing room to be used as a possible extra guest room by concealing a sink in the chest of drawers and a shower room under the stairs. After connecting the main floor to the maids' rooms, we created a guest suite in the attic space that accentuated the angles of the eaves. The client's collection of contemporary art added a humorous touch.

ABOVE AND RIGHT *By choosing well-designed furniture, such as a pair of tables by Christophe Delcourt, a prismatic table from La Galerie Italienne in Paris, and a gilt mirror by French artist Hubert le Gall, Tino made it easy and stylish. A series of lithographs by American Pop artist Roy Lichtenstein added a dynamic edge. The sofa is a Delcourt design, though slightly altered by Tino. The living room includes a number of hidden high-tech features, such as electronically controlled curtains and blinds, a beam that holds a drop-down screen and, in between the sofas, a console with a rising projector. The armchairs swivel around for convenient viewing.*

ABOVE *The small library at the end of the living room is the equivalent of a sophisticated den where the client could either work or dine. Tino designed the space paneled in limed oak and hung English artist David Hockney's drawing of his studio between the bookcases. Leather chairs from Cassina were paired with Ingo Maurer's magical light-up glass table and one of his hanging light fixtures.*

OPPOSITE *Two seating areas have been arranged for day or evening in the combination living room and study off the master bedroom. Light is controlled by a series of blinds and curtains.*

ABOVE *Tino designed the second dressing room to accommodate an extra or unexpected guest. The sofa turns into a bed. The painting is a computer enlargement from Julian Opie's* Woman Taking off…

ABOVE *To encourage weekend siestas, Tino created a large daybed that was set into the living room's bay window.*

ABOVE *With the aim to make the master bedroom as pleasant and cozy as possible, Tino used Alcantara fabric on the walls and created a small recess for the bed. He also selected well-crafted furniture, such as the bench with its chrome base, and the 1957 Di Gamma armchair by Italian architect Ignazio Gardella, which has been upholstered in black wool. The works-on-paper are from British artist Opie's 2004 silkscreen series* Bijou Gets Undressed. 4 *and* Bijou Gets Undressed. 5.

OPPOSITE *In the master bathroom, the bathtub was set on a white polished marble floor. The spiral light fixture is from Fontana Arte; the sconces are made of frosted glass and chrome, and the watery photograph by the British artist Susan Derges.*

ABOVE *The sink was recessed in an enclosure between the shower and the W.C., and in order to refine and reduce the visual impact, Tino designed the cabinet drawers in mirrored glass.*

OPPOSITE *Highlighting the curves of the guest bathroom ceiling, Tino covered the walls with mosaic tiles from Bisazza and turned the space into a grotto. The intricate tile work had to be installed on site. The designer visually enlarged the space by mirroring one of the walls.*

ABOVE *Tino designed the asymmetrical built-in headboard and book recesses, so as to have the guest room resemble a stylish stateroom on a 1930s luxury ocean liner.*

RED, WHITE, AND BLACK PIED-A-TERRE

When a two-room pied-à-terre with nine-foot-high ceilings that overlooked Manhattan's Central Park, with its ugly wood floors and exposed air-conditioning units, was bought by one of my clients, it resembled an unloved pre-war apartment. He asked me to make it modern and refined. From an architectural point of view, it was totally unprepossessing, aside from the fact that it was on the 36th floor. The views of the park were amazing. To resolve the air-conditioning issue, additional power was needed. This procedure entailed bringing a riser up from the basement, at a huge cost, but it was essential in order to make the services disappear. My idea was to give an immediate presence to the apartment with a black, red, and white color scheme, and we decided to cover the walls in Japanese washi paper panels. This gave elegance, status, and warmth because of its color and texture. We also ebonized all the new parquet floors, and added splashes of red with the furniture and art. The first piece I designed was the living room's black-and-white columned bookcase, through which one passes to reach the master bedroom and dressing room. It incorporates a secret door that gives intimacy yet saved space. In designing the kitchen, I echoed the bookcases in the living room by designing cabinets with similar half-columns. We opened up the area by mirroring the back wall and hanging a large work of art to give the effect of an enfilade. Although the apartment was compact, we were able to give it a grandeur by filling it only with elegant furniture from London, Paris, and New York antiques shops, and hanging contemporary art that reflected the color scheme. The space was so limited that it was important to have carefully selected objects and furniture to achieve the elegant scheme the client desired.

OPPOSITE *The small dining area in the kitchen can be glimpsed from the living room. Tino furnished it with a table by McCollin Bryan and the clients' Pedestal chairs designed by Eero Saarinen for Knoll.*

ABOVE LEFT *Tino emphasized the color scheme in the living room by mixing contemporary designs, such as a bronze and glass desk by Philippe Anthonioz and a Danish rug from Beauvais Carpets, a New York company, with antiques, such as late-seventeenth century Jichimu Chinese chairs and an ornate early-eighteenth century German mother-of-pearl–encrusted bureau.*

mathieu matégot

OPPOSITE *A work of art by Garry Fabian Miller, the British-born artist known for his camera-less depictions of nature, hangs above a sofa designed by Tino, and draws attention to a pair of Chinese-inspired armchairs that the designer had discreetly personalized with the owner and the owner's partner's initials.*

ABOVE *Due to the small size of the apartment, every piece of furniture was chosen to be dignified and functional.*

LEFT *American artist Steven Klein's portrait of Brad Pitt was bought by the client to complement the apartment's color scheme.*

OPPOSITE *The kitchen Tino designed was custom-made in New York. The cupboards were crafted from black-lacquered wood, and the tiles are made of dark red glass.*

COLOR, TEXTURE, AND PERSONALITY

The New York brownstone was originally configured by the English architect David Chipperfield and the English interior designer David Mlinaric, who was my partner at the time and is now retired. There were endless delays in the completion of this project due to technical difficulties and, a week before the client was to move in, a fire led to another six-month wait, during which time the furniture had to be remade. Two years later, the client, a high-powered businessman, was no longer using the ground floor and basement because neither suited his lifestyle. Since David had retired, the client asked me to return and make the unused spaces more suited to his new lifestyle. Having asked David's permission to proceed with the project, I reorganized the reception rooms by using different furniture, altering the lighting, and brought in more personality with color, texture, and more shelves to hold the client's books and belongings. Having previously worked for him, I knew the client's habits and quickly understood why he felt awkward in the ground-floor living room. There were no doors separating it from the entrance hall and, being long and narrow, it was more of an intermediate space than a room. I commissioned a translucent glass screen and placed it behind the staircase to provide a sense of privacy, while also allowing for a visual connection with the spectacular staircase. I replaced all of the more formal furniture with comfortable L-shaped sofas. The basement's dining room was too formal and Chipperfield's huge table prevented the client from moving about freely, so I replaced it with a smaller one, which relaxed the space and opened it up more to the garden—allowing him to eat dinner while watching television if he wanted to do so.

OPPOSITE *To give the house a more personalized look, Tino chose quirky pieces from the client's art collection, such as the black and white rabbit head by Nayland Blake, the American artist known for his* Negative Rabbit *series.*

ABOVE LEFT *Tino commissioned Guillaume Saalburg, the Paris-based glass artisan, to create a screen that echoed the skyline of Manhattan. As a transparent barrier, it transformed the feeling of the ground floor living room.*

ABOVE *The magnificent oak staircase designed by the English architect David Chipperfield bisects the house. The large painting is by Ugo Rondinone. The living room, at the far end of the space, is veiled, as it is behind an opaque glass screen.*

ABOVE *Since Tino's client liked living with strong color, the designer had the ottoman upholstered in orange and placed a series of pillows made from African textiles on the custom-made dark-brown velvet sofa. The circular transparent Perspex tables are by* McCollin Bryan *and the painting of an athlete is* Urinal, *a 2006 work by* Lisa Ruyter, *the Vienna, Austria-based American artist.*

LEFT *In the living room, Tino used a color scheme of chocolate brown, burnished gold, and orange to establish a masculine style. The large custom-designed, L-shaped sofas give a contemporary and cozy feel to the room. The table with the pig installation was designed by McCollin Bryan.*

BELOW LEFT *In the basement room off the garden, the round coffee table is by McCollin Bryan.*

OPPOSITE *With the oak balustrade by Chipperfield as a background, Tino set up a simple yet elegant dining area by pairing a glass-topped table from MDF Italia and Hola chairs, designed by Hannes Wettstein for Cassina in Italy. The series of panel walls were made of polished plaster. The floor is of blackened oak.*

NAUTICAL SCHEME FOR A SPORTY YACHT

When one of my longstanding clients bought a yacht, we were given seven weeks to decorate it, since he wanted to celebrate Christmas in the Caribbean—it was one of the tightest schedules we've ever had. The original design and decoration was not to his taste, as it resembled a three-star country-style hotel and felt suffocating. I imagined a blue-and-white color theme, for a sporty, nautical atmosphere. We had all the mahogany painted white so that it would lighten the feel, replaced the cheap cream-colored wool carpet with a rich dark blue linen one, which catches the light beautifully, and had the structural pillars—which appeared when we took down the wall separating the dining room from the living room—covered in dark blue leather. To compensate for the main deck's low ceilings, we created a fresh and comfortable open-plan space by removing the wall between the dining room and the salon. I also added a large sun bed on the upper deck and an extra sitting area on the back deck. The six cabins were redecorated with bed covers and curtains made of crisp cottons and linens, and we replaced the existing wall fabrics, then added the client's artwork. Since the cabin's furniture was built-in and difficult to remove, we re-styled it by changing all of the gold hardware with chrome or leather. Due to the short deadline, Antoine de Sigy, who runs my Paris office, flew down to the shipyard every week to monitor the work and construction, which took place in La Ciotat in the South of France. Although all of the fabric and furniture was shipped from Paris, the complex coordination of the project—from painting to the construction of a helipad—was organized by Composite Works. We were introduced to them by the yacht management company Hill Robinson, and the boat set sail for St. Maarten on time.

OPPOSITE *Tino replaced all of the previous furniture because, having already decorated several boats, he knew that changing the style of a sofa or the height of a chair could alter the entire look of a room. The sofa and dining room chairs on the rear deck are from Sifas in France, and are upholstered in an outdoor fabric from Perennials.*

ABOVE TOP LEFT Serena M *is a 45-meter-yacht that was built in 1996 by Pendennis Shipyard Limited, an English firm.*

ABOVE LEFT *To create the sun bed on the top deck, Tino assembled six mattresses from Kettal and upholstered them in an outdoor fabric from Perennials that would stand up to the sea air.*

LEFT *In the small entry vestibule on the starboard side, the white-painted woodwork and white linen wallcovering is offset by the shimmering dark-blue linen carpet. A glass console and mirror by Fontana Arte hang on the wall. An ink drawing of a telephone by American artist Donald Baechler and an unexpected sheep sculpture lend an element of surprise.*

BELOW LEFT *In the master bedroom, Tino hung pieces from the client's art collection, including a series by American artist Jenny Holzer,* above bed, *and a photograph by the American David LaChapelle,* right. *The dark-blue linen carpet was specially dyed and woven for the yacht. Originally, Tino wanted it to be made of silk but time constraints made that impossible.*

RIGHT *In the dining area, an aquatic work by French artist Didier Massard has been hung near the large recessed mirror.*

OVERLEAF *To warm up the feeling of the main salon, Tino designed armchairs, sofas, and an ottoman, which are upholstered in a fabric from Holland & Sherry. The striped linen pillows are from Caravane. Fitting in with boat regulations, every piece of furniture had to be fixed to the floor by Composite Works, and all the fabrics were fire treated. The pair of aquarium-like works of art is by Julian Opie.*

Index

Photograph Credits

Andrew Beasley: 128-135
Antoine Bootz: 114-127, 156-171
Leonardo Cosa: 174-185
Jacques Dirand: 21
Photography by Andreas von Einsiedel: 218-221, 224-225
Marili Forastieri: 242-247
Reto Guntli: 28-29, 102-107
Marianne Haas: 1-2, 4, 6, 8, 10, 12-13, 15, 26-27, 30-35, 38-81, 84-101, 108-113, 138-147, 148-155, 190-191, 198, 226-235, 257
Hugh Henry: 36-37, 82-83, 136-137, 172-173, 216-217
Vincent Knapp: 8
Nick Johnson: 236-241
Derry Moore: 6, 24-26
Nobuaki Nakagawa: 201-203, 206-215
Julien Oppenheim: 222-223
Vangelis Paterakis—www.studiopaterakis.com: 186-189, 192-197, 199
Yuki Sugahara: 200, 204-205
Photography by Bruce Thomas, yamayamaghts.com: 248-253
Tino Zervudachi private collection: 16-20, 22

Dedication & acknowledgments

This book is dedicated to Louis-Charles, for his patience in accommodating my impossible work and travel schedules, as well as my exhausted humor as a result; and also to my family, notably my parents Carolyn and Nolly, my twin sister Manuela, and my uncle Marke and aunt Jacqui, all of whose unconditional support has always been inspiring and energizing.

Special thanks to David Mlinaric, without whom I would not have become a decorator at all. I am forever grateful for his continual patience and encouragement, and also for his thoughtfulness and generosity in the Foreword; to Lindy Guinness, for her very kind preface, her friendship, and her talent.

A big thank you to all of my clients—past, present, and future—for giving me the opportunity to create their homes, and especially to those who have allowed me to include their houses in this book, and have graciously agreed to be interviewed. I also thank all of their representatives, assistants, and secretaries for their help and patience throughout the laborious decoration processes.

Thank you to my endlessly supportive friends, too numerous to mention by name. A special thank you to all those who have been involved in the making of this book, which was so much more work than I could have possibly imagined: Natasha Fraser-Cavassoni, for her insightful text; Marianne Haas, who travelled to far-flung places to get these projects done with me (and what fun we had!); Andrew Beasley, Antoine Bootz, Pascal Chevallier, Leonardo Costa, Jacques Dirand, Andreas Von Einsiedel, Marili Forastieri, Reto Guntli, Nick Johnson, Vincent Knapp, Nobuaki Nakagawa, Julien Oppenheim, Vangelis Paterakis, and Bruce Thomas for their beautiful photography.

To Suzanne Slesin, my publisher and editor, Stafford Cliff, the talented art director, Dominick J. Santise, Jr., and the whole team at Pointed Leaf Press, including Regan Toews, Deanna Kawitzky, Nyasha Gutsa, and Marion D.S. Dreyfus.

To everyone in my office in Paris, who has helped with the book and has made these projects come to life: Marie Leroux, who has been invaluable to us all in organizing the contents of this book; Antoine de Sigy; Dennis Pyle; and Marie-Astrid Piron.

To my office in London: my partner, Hugh Henry, for his beautiful watercolors for the chapter headings; Jason Roberts, Laurence Macadam, Nina Benhissen, Chris Miners, and the rest of the team, past and present, for all their work in getting these projects finished.

To Yuki Sugahara in Tokyo, for all her invaluable work on the Japanese projects; to Diane Burgio and Nicole Porter in New York, for their help and patience; and to Afranio Cunha, for our work in Rio de Janeiro. I would like to thank the architects I have worked with on these projects: Laurent Bourgois, David Connors, Tony Collett, Tim Hatton, Kengo Kuma, Eva Mavrakis, Luciano Pedrosa, Torres Torres, Bruno Jori, and Theodore Zoumboulakis. Thank you to all of the landscape architects: Miranda Brooks, Louis Benech, Martin Lane Fox, and François Goffinet.

A big thank you to all of the artists, artisans, contractors, and suppliers that I collaborated with. In France, I thank Philippe Anthonioz, Nicolas Aubagnac, Dominique Bouillon, Jean-Pierre Bouvet, Maison Boyer, Rémy Brazet, Christine Brossard (Aissa Dione), Capeline, Stéphane Chapelle, Maison Charles, Laurent Chwast, Cousins Associés (La Sosegh), Passementerie Declerq (Catherine Magnier), Christophe Delcourt, Deport Frères, Galerie Diurne (Marcel Zelmanovitch), Dunod Mallier, André Dubreuil, François-Xavier Dutruc-Rosset, FBZ BVBA (Bartholomeus), Gander & White, Etablissements Gérald, G.M.T., Florence Girette, Vincent Guerre, Menuiserie Guitton, Andrew Hartley & Stéphanie Tissier, Holland & Sherry, Ateliers Joël Joubert, Agnès Laethem, Leinis (Philippe Legros), Le Manach, Jean-François Lesage, Librairie Galignani, Librairie 7L, Le Lit National, Atelier de la Main d'Or, Malleville, Didier Massard, Ingo Maurer, Catherine Meilleur, Entreprise Montagnier, Laurence Montano, Pierre Moulin, Christian Mussy, Joel Orgiazzi, CB Parsua (Céline Letessier), Jean-Paul Phelippeau and Alain Simonnot, Piermar (Dominique Lingerie), Pouenat, Manufacture Prelle, Valérie Rebelo, Rogers & Goffigon, Renard (Brigitte Montaut), Roussel Stores, Jean Roze, Jennifer Shorto, Guillaume Saalburg, Style Décoration (Philippe Leger), S.O.E., Tassinari et Chatel, Vincent Vanechop, Composite Works, and Manuela Zervudachi. In England, 800 Group, McCollin Bryan, Claremont, Christopher Farr, Gerratts, Howard Chairs, Rory Howard, Interior Workshop Killigrew King, Simon Peers, R&M Curtains, and Pierre Vuillemenot. In Greece, Diane Sedden. In the U.S., Beauvais Carpets and De Angelis Furniture. In Japan, T.C.K.W. In Brazil, Afranio Cunha, Mi Casa, and Esther Giobbi. In Italy, Antico Setificio Fiorentino. In Switzerland, Claude Schaer and Nathalie Zervudachi.

Thank you to all the galleries and art dealers. In France, Galerie Arcanes, Galerie Bazin, Jean-François de Blanchetti, Antoine Brocardo, Galerie Chevalier, Jean-François Dubois, Laurent Dubois, Galerie Camoin-Demachy (Edouard Demachy), Galerie Dutko, Galerie Flore, Galerie Patrick Fourtin, Galerie Yves Gastou, Galerie Golovanoff, Philippe Guegan, H.P. Le Studio, Galerie Jacques Lacoste, Jacques Lafon, Galerie Andrée Macé, Edouard de La Marque, Galerie Jean-Gabriel Mitterand, Galerie Montluc, Laurent Moreux, Gladys Mougin, Philippe Murat-David, Eric Philippe, Danbon Pokorny, François and Christine Pouillon, Lionel Sanderson, Philippe Sinceux, Louis Soubrier, Jean Wanecq, and Galerie Olivier Watelet. In England, Jean Claude Ciancimino, Hemisphere Design Gallery, and Piers von Westenholz. In Greece, the Peggy Zoumboulakis Gallery. In Switzerland, Urs von Unger.

Tino Zervudachi—December 2011

Natasha Fraser-Cavassoni is a Paris-based British writer who has been covering interiors and lifestyle for twenty years. She began at *W Magazine*, then became the European Editor of *Harper's Bazaar*, and now contributes to such publications as *Architectural Digest*, *Elle Decor* and *The International Herald Tribune*. In addition to writing the bi-monthly column "Inner Chic" for *Another Magazine*, she is the author of *Sam Spiegel: The Biography of A Hollywood Legend*, *Understanding Chic*, an essay from the *Paris Was Ours* anthology, and the *Chanel Book*, for Assouline's fashion series.

ENDPAPERS *Loose drawings and notes by Tino Zervudachi are part of his design process.*

HALF-TITLE PAGE *A nineteenth-century plaster cast of an original sculpture in the Louvre Museum of the Egyptian pharaoh, Ramses II, stands in the entrance of the office in Paris.*

OPPOSITE TITLE PAGE *In an eighteenth-century hôtel particulier in Paris, a glass-topped table with a gilded-iron base echoes the curves of the spoon-back chairs designed by Tino Zervudachi.*

OPPOSITE TABLE OF CONTENTS *In the main living space of a house in Greece, Tino Zervudachi had the walls painted white and the heavy wood beams a pale grey-blue.*

OPPOSITE *The Paris office of Mlinaric, Henry & Zervudachi overlooks the Jardins du Palais-Royal.*

Mlinaric, Henry & Zervudachi S.A.S.
44, Rue Saint Anne, 75002 Paris
T: + 33 (0) 1 42 96 08 62
F: + 33 (0) 1 42 97 44 92
E: info@mhzparis.com
www.mhzparis.com

Mlinaric, Henry & Zervudachi Ltd.
38 Bourne Street, London SWIW 8JA
T: + 44 (0) 207 730 9072
F: + 44 (0) 207 823 4756
E: info@mhzlondon.com
www.mhzlondon.com

Pointed Leaf Press, LLC.
136 Baxter Street, New York, NY 10013
www.pointedleafpress.com

Pointed Leaf Press is pleased to offer special discounts for our publications. We also create special edition copies and can provide signed copies upon request. Please contact info@pointedleafpress.com for details or visit our website at www.pointedleafpress.com.

Printed and bound in China
First edition
10 9 8 7 6 5 4 3 2
Library of Congress Control Number: 2011944796
ISBN 13: 9780983388968

125cm
135cm
75cm
plateau en cuir
cimaise
cuir
parchemin
bois vernis à l'interieur (sur les côtés)
≃ 55H x 90L x 35P
PARCHMENT SIDE TABLES FOR EITHER SIDE OF SOFA
very light unlined linen curtains with hooks as living room
plan